P9-CBA-820

Seasons of Praise

Seasons of Praise

A 52-Week Worship Celebration for the Entire Family

REBECCA HAYFORD BAUER

VICTOR BOOKS
A Division of Scripture Press Publications Inc.

All Scripture is paraphrased by the author to be understandable by young children.

Editor: Barbara Williams
Art Director: Andrea Boven
Cover Calligraphy: Timothy Botts
Illustrator: Rebecca Bauer
Production: Myrna Hasse, Andrea Boven
Back Cover and Flap Photo: Christopher Glenn Photography

ISBN: 1-56476-582-2
Suggested Subject Heading: Gift, Inspirational

Printed in the United States of America.

1 2 3 4 5 6 7 8 9 10 Printing/Year 00 99 98 97 96

For information write Victor Books, 1825 College Avenue, Wheaton, Illinois 60187

Contents

Acknowledgments

As with any project, it never reaches completion without the help of may others.

Thank you to Christa Hayford Andersen (the world's most awesome sister), Susanne Mahdi, and Diana Neciosup-Acuna for their constant encouragement and editorial help. They along with Christine Amerson and Gunta Irbe bore this project and me in prayer for many months.

Thank you to Michelle Glush and Bob Dawson who helped me make sure everything looked good—artistically and musically.

A very special thank you to Cindy Henderson who helped with almost every part of this project—editing, praying, encouraging, and laying out the music.

Thank you to Dr. Tom McDonald, Dawn Loomis, and Gary Howse for their help in supplying resources for research.

Thank you again to the staff at Victor Books, especially Dave Horton and Andrea Boven. (And to the production team . . . I promise to never use that blue pencil again!)

Thank you to my husband, Scott, and my children, Brian, Kyle, and Lindsey. Without your help and support, I would never get anything completed! Now that this book is completed, I promise to tackle the ironing!

And thank you to my daughter, Lindsey, for helping me complete one beautiful border!
(See page 60.)

Finally, thank You Lord, for helping me with a project that turned out to be very physically demanding. I've learned a new dimension of relying only on Your strength!

> *Psalm 44:3—"For they did not gain possession of the land by their own sword, nor did their own arm save them, but it was Your right hand, Your arm, and the light of Your countenance" (NKJV).*

To my husband,

Scott

Thank you for your constant prayer—
when you pray for me, God answers!

Thank you for your complete support—
I could never do anything without you!

And thank you for your unconditional love.
The Lord did a good thing when He put us together;
I love you with all of my heart!

Introduction

If there were only two things that I would long for every family to incorporate into the life, atmosphere, and experience of their home they would be, without question, worship and the Word.

I'm not talking about application of these practices that turns people into religious "weirdos" who aren't fully connected to reality. I'm talking about an experience with the Lord Jesus Christ that is so real and vital that it penetrates every part of a family's life. Why are these two dimensions of our walk with the Lord so crucial to home life? Because, when applied faithfully, they secure the stability of our homes. *The Word* provides us with solid truth that gives us a sure foundation on which to build our lives and our homes. *Worship* allows us to live in the light and joy of God's presence, banishing the "shifting sands" of the world and the assaults of the adversary that seek to destroy and divide families.

INVITING GOD'S PRESENCE THROUGH WORSHIP

Scripture teaches us that worship actually invites the presence of God. "But You are holy, *enthroned in the praises of Israel*" (Ps. 22:3). So, when we worship the Lord, we are actually welcoming Him to be where we are—not just as our Savior, but as our King. The idea that God wants to live with us in our homes isn't new. Isaiah reveals that God's true desire is for His presence to dwell over every home: "Then the Lord will create *above every dwelling place*... a cloud and smoke by day and the shining of a flaming fire by night. For over *all* the glory there will be a covering" (4:5).

God's presence is always available to His people. But the Lord, being the gentleman He is, will never intrude where He isn't invited. Just as He didn't force His way into our hearts to provide salvation, He will not force His daily presence upon us. So lift your voice in worship to willingly welcome Him ... He's just waiting for the invitation.

Worship through music is also a powerful teaching tool!

Praise music is a resource that can instill godly principles, memory verses, and faith-building concepts into the minds and hearts of our children in such a way that they will never be forgotten!

We've all had it happen! We hear an "oldie but goodie" on the radio and it's as if we're transported back in time! We can remember lyrics instantly—even if we haven't heard them in years! We can do the same thing for our children. As we teach them the songs of the Lord, we are engraving God's Word on their hearts.

ESTABLISHING A FIRM FOUNDATION THROUGH THE WORD

Scripture also tells us that the Word of God will stand forever (Isa. 40:8; Matt. 5:18; 24:35; 1 Peter 1:25). When we apply the principles of God's Word to every aspect of our homes and relationships, we are building on an unshakable, uncompromising foundation that will never be destroyed. For a quick look at what the Word does in our lives, read through Psalm 119. Some feature of God's Word is pointed out in every verse of that psalm.

Of course, having a head knowledge of the Word and playing worship tapes in your home is merely scratching the surface. God wants us to move from head knowledge: to heart knowledge to a place where His Word literally becomes a part of who we are—a vital, living influence that calls forth our pure, genuine, and sincere worship.

LIVING THE WORD

As adults, we can mentally comprehend these concepts and apply them to our lives, but how do we teach our children to live God's Word?

First, the power of a regular devotional habit can never be underestimated. This can be applied in a variety of ways. Some families have a daily family worship; others find that impractical. Some families discuss portions of the Word, play Bible games, or go over Sunday School handouts. All of these have a place, and at different times in our family's life, we have done them all! However you apply it, teach your children to read the Word . . . and *you* do the same. Then, as the Lord brings about natural opportunities, talk about how the Word applies to our lives.

The second way children learn how to live God's Word is by watching us. This is the most sobering aspect of parenthood: the fact that our children imitate everything we do—the good and the beautiful . . . and the bad and the ugly! But Jesus calls us to live in such a way that our children can "follow us as we follow Christ" (1 Cor. 11:1). Let us walk with the Lord in such a way that we can boldly declare with Paul, "I *urge* you to imitate me!" (4:16)

A third way that we can teach our children how the Word lives in us is by learning about the lives of other believers. From telling them about God's workings in *your* life to learning about the "heroes of faith" in past centuries, God means for us to be an inspiration to one another! Hebrews 12:1 says, "Since we are surrounded by so many witnesses who have successfully lived their Christian walk before us, let us be encouraged to lay aside everything that holds us back, and every sin that so easily traps us, and run with endurance the race that is before us."

As you use this book to fulfill the command of Deuteronomy 6:6-7, may you have as many joyous conversations with your children about the life-giving, life-changing, and life-fulfilling power of worship and the Word in your home as we have had in ours!

> *"And these words which I command you today shall be in your heart; you shall teach them diligently to your children, and shall talk of them when you sit in your house, when you walk by the way, when you lie down, and when you rise up" (Deut. 6:6-7).*

Foreword

As a missionary child in Argentina, family devotional time was as regular as breakfast. There were many days when we five children came dragging into the living room, dreading what my little sister called "votions." Dad had the ability, however, to make biblical accounts come to life. We stood with arms held out as long as we could, pretending to be Moses at the battle of the Amalekites. We acted out the story of the Good Samaritan, lying on the floor, groaning in pain, waiting for the hero of the story to stop and help. Sometimes we sang, harmonizing and blending our voices in songs of adoration and praise.

What I did not realize at the time, was that I was getting a taste of the Lord's goodness. When we sang, prayed, worshiped, and listened, we were being changed by God's presence. Even though I could not describe the feeling, there was something transcendent taking place. Years later, as a prodigal, God used the foundation of those precious family times to draw me back to Himself.

Today, Marijean and I have found great joy in seeing our own children come to faith in Christ and begin to develop an intimate love relationship with Him. One of the means God has used is our devotional times as a family.

Rebecca Hayford Bauer is no stranger to worship. She comes from a rich heritage of vital faith and ministry. It is not surprising that God would use her to provide families with such a valuable resource. *Seasons of Praise* is the spark to ignite your family worship times. Each theme, devotional, and song, helps direct hearts to the fountain of life, Jesus Christ.

What a blessing awaits those whose home is filled with praise and delight in the Lord!

STEVE GREEN

How To Use This Book

Dear Parent,

Our quest as parents to institute family worship often breeds only frustration or condemnation. The demands and realities of our society (dual-parent work schedules, long commutes, and single-parent families) put time with our families at a premium. And the technological invasion of our homes through faxes, cell phones, and beepers can put us at the beck and call of others 'round the clock. Yet, as difficult as finding that time may be, worshiping the Lord together as a family can be very fulfilling, life-giving, unifying, and growth-producing.

Seasons of Praise provides a time-effective, relationship-building way to establish regular family worship by providing a resource for a weekly time of worship with your children, through three distinct features:

Feature 1:

A monthly theme to give each month's times of sharing a structure and purpose. Use the book by the month or by the theme.

Feature 2:

A weekly devotional to equip parents in communicating their faith to their children through the use of biblical truth and personal testimony. These examples can inspire discussion on how to live daily with the Lord as we see how others have met the challenges of living a life of faith.

Feature 3:

Meaningful worship music, via hymns and choruses, that will add to the joy in any home, reinforce the lessons learned, and plant eternal truths in children's hearts.

As you move through the book, adjust it to your family's life. Often a topic comes up naturally with children. Don't wait until that month comes around! Go directly to that month and apply the theme while their minds and hearts are ready to receive the information!

Then, our calendars being what they are, there is an "extra week" in each three-month period. To accommodate this, one extra devotional has been added at the end of each quarter—in March, June, September, and December. But if that extra week doesn't come in one of those months this year, take the extra devotional and apply it elsewhere!

Other weeks are marked specifically for certain holidays—like Easter or Thanksgiving. But some holidays don't fall in the same month every year, let alone on the same date! So, be flexible and move the devotionals around to suit the current year and your family's immediate interests.

January: Our Foundation

Have you ever tried to imagine "forever"? It seems pretty hard. Have you ever thought about things that last forever? Stop right now and tell your mom or dad what you think will last forever.

What did you say? Maybe you think the world will last forever. Maybe you think Superman will last forever. Some days, maybe you think school will last forever! Those things really won't last forever, but the Bible tells us something that will: God's Word.

"The Word of the Lord lasts forever" (1 Peter 1:25). Jesus says that heaven and earth will someday end, "but My words will never go away" (Matt. 24:35).

What makes this most amazing is that a large part of the Bible is made up of promises God has made to us! If God's Word will last forever, that means that the promises God has made to us will last too! They will never fail us (1 Kings 8:56; Ps. 111:7; Ezek. 12:25).

That's what this hymn is about. No one knows for sure who wrote the hymn, "How Firm a Foundation," but we *do* know that its original title was "Exceeding great and precious promises." That phrase is taken from another Bible verse, 2 Peter 1:4, that talks about all of the wonderful promises the Lord has given us through Jesus.

What do you need a promise from the Lord for? No matter what it is, I guarantee you that God has a promise for it in the Bible. Here are just a few to get you started!

When you're happy: When the Lord comforts us, He brings joy, gladness, thanksgiving, and singing into our lives! (Isa. 51:3) We are to rejoice always (Phil. 4:4).

If you have a test: You are to run a race so well that you will win! (1 Cor. 9:24) (In this case, it means to study!) Jesus promises to "bring to mind" what we've learned (John 14:26).

If you're afraid: God isn't the one who makes us afraid (2 Tim. 1:7), so when you are afraid, use the sword of the Word of God (Eph. 6:17) and fight back with these verses: Psalms 91:5; 118:6; Proverbs 3:24; Isaiah 41:10; Acts 18:9; Hebrews 13:6; 1 Peter 3:14.

When other kids are mean to you: No one suffered more unfairness than David did. You can read about his life in 1 and 2 Samuel, and some of the lessons he learned (Pss. 59:16-17; 20:1; 5:11).

If you need to forgive: We need to forgive others in the same way that we have been forgiven by God (Eph. 4:32).

When peer pressure is really pressing in: Read the story of Shadrach, Meshach, and Abed-nego in the fiery furnace (Dan. 3). The Lord protected them and honored them for standing firm in following Him.

When you feel lonely or you're the new kid: Jesus "will never leave you nor forsake you" (Heb. 13:5), and God will be with us and take care of us wherever we are (Gen. 28:15).

Just think—all of these promises will last forever! Which promise do you need to use today?

How Firm a Foundation

Rippon's Selection of Hymns
Traditional American Melody
Coldwell's Union Harmony
1. How firm a foun - da - tion, ye saints of the Lord,
2. "Fear not, I am with thee; O be not dis - mayed,
3. "When through the deep wat - ters I call thee to go,
4. "When through fier - y tri - als thy path - way shall lie,
5. "The soul that on Je - sus hath leaned for re - pose,
Is laid for your faith in His ex - cel - lent Word!
For I am thy God, and will still give thee aid;
The riv - ers of sor - row shall not o - ver - flow;
My grace, all suf - fi - cient, shall be thy sup - ply:
I will not, I will not de - sert to his foes;
What more can He say than to you He hath said,
I'll strength - en thee, help thee, and cause thee to stand,
For I will be with thee, thy trou - bles to bless,
The flame shall not hurt thee; I on - ly de - sign
That soul, though all hell should en - deav - or to shake,
To you who for ref - uge to Je - sus have fled?
Up - held by my right - eous, om - nip - o - tent hand.
And sanc - ti - fy to thee thy deep - est dis - tress.
Thy dross to con - sume, and thy gold to re - fine.
I'll nev - er, no, nev - er, no, nev - er for - sake!" A - men.
FROSTY THE SNOWMAN

About fifty years after the Pilgrims landed at Plymouth, there was a young man in Germany who was far away from God. One Sunday he decided to go to a church service just to make fun of everything that was going on. Instead, the words of the preacher reached his heart and he came to know the Lord. His name was Joachim Neander and he wrote the song, "Praise to the Lord, the Almighty."

This song begins by telling us that not only is Jesus the foundation of our lives, but He is also "the King of Creation." You probably already knew that! Genesis 1:1 is one of the first verses you learn in Sunday School: "In the beginning God created the heavens and the earth." But did you know that the Bible also says that God created all things "through Jesus Christ"? (Eph. 3:9) It tells us that "everything was made through the Word" (John 1:3) and "by [Jesus] all things were created that are in heaven and earth" (Col. 1:16). Jesus really is the King of Creation!

Do you know *why* Creation was given to us? First of all, God has given us "all things to enjoy" (1 Tim. 6:17). God wants us to enjoy what He has made for us! Second, Creation was given to us to teach us about the Lord. Since Creation, God's traits are able to be seen (Rom. 1:20). Let's look at some of the things God teaches us through Creation.

The Lord teaches us about His forgiveness through the beauty of snow: "Though your sins are like scarlet, they shall be as white as snow" (Isa. 1:18). The skies declare God's glory and show us His work (Ps. 19:1). If we follow God's commands, we will flourish and grow like a tree that receives abundant water (1:3). Jesus said that our connection to Him is as close as a vine and a branch (John 15:5). The Lord promises blessings to come like rain (Ezek. 34:26), and that He will be like the dew to His people—new and refreshing every day (Hosea 14:5). The Lord will protect us like a wall of fire (Zech. 2:5), and He will give us "living water" so that our hearts will never thirst again—we will be filled with Him (John 4:14).

Another part of God's creation is YOU! And He loves you a lot! God cares so much about you that He knows exactly how many hairs are on your head (Matt. 10:30). When you are sad, He keeps your tears in a bottle, because everything about you is valuable to God (Ps. 56:8). Your name is written on God's hands (Isa. 49:16), and God calls you one of His jewels (Mal. 3:17).

King Solomon writes, "Remember your Creator when you are young" (Ecc. 12:1). Just like this song invites us to praise the Lord, we need to remember all the wonderful things our Creator has done. Look around at God's creation and see in its beauty the beauty of the Lord, and then praise Him with all of your heart.

Praise to the Lord, the Almighty

Joachim Neander
Ernewerten Gesangbuch
1 Praise to the Lord, the Al - might - y, the King of cre - a - tion! O my soul, praise him, for he is your health and sal - va - tion! Let all who hear Now to his tem - ple draw near, Join - ing in glad ad - o - ra - tion!
2 Praise to the Lord, who o'er all things is won - drous - ly reign - ing And, as on wings of an ea - gle, up - lift - ing, sus - tain - ing. Have you not seen All that is need - ful has been Sent by his gra - cious or - dain - ing?
3 Praise to the Lord, who will pros - per your work and de - fend you; Sure - ly his good - ness and mer - cy shall dai - ly at - tend you. Pon - der a - new What the Al - might - y can do If with his love he be - friend you.
4 Praise to the Lord! Oh, let all that is in me a - dore him! All that has life and breath, come now with prais - es be - fore him! Let the a - men Sound from his peo - ple a - gain. Glad - ly for - ev - er a - dore him!
FROSTY THE SNOWMAN

Imagine you just woke up on a cold January morning! Brrrr! You don't even want to get out of bed, it's so cold! Then Mom calls you for breakfast. You're still not too interested in facing the cold, but maybe a cup of hot chocolate would lure you out!

Now imagine that Mom made that cup of hot chocolate for you, but only filled the cup halfway—then filled it the rest of the way with water. Doesn't sound so good now, does it? Watered down hot chocolate is disappointing in how good it tastes, how good it looks, and how good it is for you.

In the middle 1800s that is what several leaders in the Church of England were trying to do with the Bible. They were saying that the Bible wasn't correct in the facts it gave, that the miracles of the Bible couldn't possibly be believed, and that it was really just a group of nice stories. They were trying to explain Creation through evolution, which was a brand-new idea then. And they were putting a lot of confusion in people's minds about the truth of God's Word. Over a period of several years, this became a huge argument with many people questioning: Was the Bible true or not?

This is just like the hot chocolate! These men were trying to "water down" the beliefs of the church. And, just like hot chocolate, once our faith is watered down, it doesn't "taste" or look as good, and it certainly isn't as good for you!

In the middle of this big argument, Samuel Stone, a pastor, wrote the song "The Church's One Foundation." He wanted to remind everyone that the foundation of our faith is Jesus Christ. If we don't believe the Bible, then our faith has no meaning. If we don't believe that the Bible truthfully reports miracles, then the miracle of Jesus being the Son of God could never be true. Our faith in Jesus Christ requires us to also place our faith in what God's Word teaches us.

Through this song, Samuel reminded people that you can have faith in all kinds of things—science, evolution, and arguments. Some people even put their faith in doubt and disbelief by saying they don't believe in God, by challenging all authority, or by being negative. But if you're going to be one of God's people, you have to put your faith completely in Jesus Christ and everything that He stands for, and the Bible which faithfully tells us about Him. In 1 Corinthians 3:11, the Apostle Paul tells us:

> *There is no other foundation that anyone can build except that which is already built—Jesus Christ.*

That's where I want to put my faith! How about you?

The Church's One Foundation

Samuel J. Stone
Samuel S. Wesley
1. The Church's one foun - da - tion Is Je - sus Christ her Lord;
2. E - lect from ev - 'ry na - tion, Yet one o'er all the earth,
3. Though with a scorn-ful won - der Men see her sore op - pressed,
4. 'Mid toil and trib - u - la - tion, And tu - mult of her war,
5. Yet she on earth hath un - ion With God, the Three in One,
She is His new cre - a - tion, By wa - ter and the word;
Her char - ter of sal - va - tion, One Lord, one faith, one birth;
By schisms rent a - sun - der, By her - e - sies dis - tressed:
She waits the con-sum - ma - tion Of peace for - ev - er - more;
And mys - tic sweet com - mun - ion With those whose rest is won:
From heav'n He came and sought her to be His ho - ly bride;
One ho - ly name she bless - es, Par - takes one ho - ly food,
Yet saints their watch are keep - ing, Their cry goes up, "How long?"
Till with the vi - sion glo - rious Her long - ing eyes are blest,
O hap - py ones and ho - ly! Lord, give us grace that we,
With His own blood He bought her, And for her life He died.
And to one hope she press - es, With ev - 'ry grace en - dued.
And soon the night of weep - ing Shall be the morn of song.
And the great Church vic - to - rious Shall be the Church at rest.
Like them, the meek and low - ly, On high may dwell with Thee. A-men.
FROSTY THE SNOWMAN

They drank of that spiritual Rock... and that Rock was Christ. 1 Cor. 10:4

Ascribe greatness to our God... He is the rock. Deut. 32:3,4

The Lord is my rock and my fortress and my deliverer. Ps. 18:2.

Behold, a king will reign in righteousness... as the shadow of a great rock in a weary land. Isa. 32:1,2

Lead me to the rock that is higher than I. Ps. 61:2

That Rock is Christ!

A young boy grows up in a godless home, unaware that a loving God even exists. His Sundays are spent roaming the streets looking for anything to keep his mind off of his loneliness and boredom. His school doesn't allow the Bible to be *seen*, let alone taught. Sound familiar? This was what the childhood of Edward Mote was like in the early 1800s.

We tend to think that people have turned against God only in our generation and that it's too bad we can't live in "the good ol' days." But the things that make people do good or evil always stay the same. Almost 3,000 years ago, Solomon wrote, "There is nothing new under the sun" (Ecc. 1:9). He knew what he was talking about, because the story is always the same: without God, people become more and more sinful.

When Edward was sixteen, his boss took him to a church service where, for the first time, he heard the message of salvation. He responded instantly, and from that moment, Edward's life took on purpose: he was going to serve Jesus Christ! And he did! First as a young businessman, and later as the pastor of a church.

Throughout his life, Edward sought to teach people about the foundation and purpose Jesus Christ can bring to their lives. Edward knew all about that because he had grown up with the unsteadiness and insecurity of the world's way of living. He knew it didn't offer anything solid to build his life on. Many years after his conversion, he wrote the song "The Solid Rock" to describe "the gracious experience of a Christian."

Edward's experience reminds us of a story that Jesus told. Jesus describes a wise man who built his house on a rock and a foolish man who built his house on the sand (Matt. 7:24-29). Then a storm came! The rain pounded down and flood waters rose dangerously high. The wind blew ferociously against both houses. Of course, the house on the rock was not only on higher ground that protected it from the flood waters, but its foundation was solidly built. That house stood secure! The other house, however, had a shifting foundation because it was built only on sand. So as the sand moved underneath it from the floods and wind, that house fell down because it wasn't built on something solid.

In the same way, we make a choice about what we are going to build *our* lives on. We can build our lives on the "sands" of the world that don't offer anything firm. Or we can choose to build our lives on the foundation of the Rock of Jesus Christ.

The "sands" of the world change based on things that don't last—like friends, money, or ideas. They also shift because of the "storms" that come along in life—things that make us afraid or uncertain. But when we build our lives on Jesus, no matter what storm comes along, we know that we can stand firm. Jesus said:

"Anyone who hears My sayings and does them, is like a wise man who builds his house on the rock: the rains come, the floods come, and the winds blow, but the house won't fall, because it's founded on the rock" (Matt. 7:24-25).

The Solid Rock

Edward Mote William B. Bradbury

1. My hope is built on noth - ing less Than Je - sus' blood and
2. When dark - ness veils His love - ly face, I rest on His un -
3. His oath, His cov - e - nant, His blood Sup - port me in the
4. When He shall come with trum - pet sound, O may I then in
right - eous - ness; I dare not trust the sweet - est frame, But
chang - ing grace; In ev - 'ry high and storm - y gale, My
whelm - ing flood; When all a - round my soul gives way He
Him be found; Dressed in His right - eous - ness a - lone, Fault -
whol - ly lean on Je - sus' name.
an - chor holds with - in the vale.
then is all my hope and stay.
less to stand be - fore the throne.
Refrain
On Christ the sol - id Rock I stand; All oth - er ground is sink - ing sand. All oth - er ground is sink - ing sand.
FROSTY THE SNOWMAN

February: Love

There is no truth in the Bible as amazing and life changing as the simple fact that God loves us. Out of that love, He made the supreme sacrifice of His Son so that we could receive His great and awesome love.

This simple song, "Jesus Loves Me," reminds us of the fact that God loves us, and assures us that we can be *certain* of God's love because "the Bible tells me so." The promise is written there for us to read and hold onto and learn about. Most amazing is the fact that God chose to love us simply because we are His creation. We don't have to do something spectacular or be anything other than who we are for Him to pour out His love on us. God's love has been described as "unconditional" love. That means that when we make a mistake or fail at something, even when we're not sure we like ourselves—God *still* loves us! We can count on the fact that God's love will always be there. It will never, ever change or go away.

Have you ever read the "love" verses in the Bible? Here are a few that tell us how much God loves us.

- God shows His love for us in this way: *while we were still sinners*, Jesus died for us! (Rom. 5:8)
- In His love and in His mercy God rescued us (Isa. 63:9).
- There is no greater love than this: that someone gives his life for his friends (John 15:13).
- This is love: not that we loved God, but that He loved us and sent His Son to die for our sins (1 John 4:10).
- God loved the world so much that He gave His only Son, so that if anyone believes in Him, he won't die but have eternal life (John 3:16).
- Because of His great love for us, God, who is rich in mercy, made us alive with Christ when we were spiritually dead in our sins—it is by grace you have been saved (Eph. 2:4-5).
- Do you know how great God's love for us is? He even calls us His *children*! (1 John 3:1)
- I have loved you with an everlasting love (Jer. 31:3).
- Nothing can separate us from God's love . . . not death nor life, not angels nor demons, not what's happening now nor what's going to happen in the future, not any powers, not things up high, or things down low, not anything in all of creation. None of these things will ever be able to separate us from the love of God that is in Christ Jesus our Lord (Rom. 8:38-39).

Isn't it nice to be loved!

HI

Jesus Loves Me

Anna B. Warner
William B. Bradbury
1. Je - sus loves me! this I know, For the Bi - ble tells me so;
2. Je - sus loves me! He who died Heav - en's gate to o - pen wide;
3. Je - sus loves me! He will stay Close be - side me all the way;
Lit - tle ones to Him be - long, They are weak but He is strong.
He will wash a - way my sin, Let His lit - tle child come in.
Thou hast bled and died for me, I will hence - forth live for Thee.
Refrain
Yes, Je - sus loves me! Yes, Je - sus loves me!
Yes, Je - sus loves me! The Bi - ble tells me so.

Is there someone you just love being around? When you're with them you feel loved and encouraged. You learn things from them and have lots of fun with them. Maybe it's Gramma or Grampa. Maybe it's your teacher or an aunt or uncle. Maybe it's a close friend. Maybe it's Mom or Dad. It doesn't matter *who* it is—you just *love* to be around them.

That's how King David felt about the Lord when he wrote; "There's only one thing I want from the Lord, and that's the one thing I'm going to ask for: I want to live in the house of the Lord my whole life, so that I can see His beauty, and grow to know Him in His temple" (Ps. 27:4).

That is the same verse that a twelve-year-old boy named Don underlined in his Bible shortly after he asked Jesus into his heart. Years later, after Don Moen had grown up, he wrote about that same desire in the song, "I Want to Be Where You Are."

Don had been reading about a very sad event in Exodus 20:18-21. When Moses had led the people of Israel to Mount Sinai, God had promised to give them His Law. But before He did, He told Israel that they had to prepare to meet with Him. So the people of Israel spent three days cleaning their tents, purifying their bodies, and preparing their hearts to come into God's presence.

The great day finally arrived and God came down to Mount Sinai. When He came, there was the sound of thunder and a great trumpet. There was also lightning and all of Mount Sinai was covered with smoke. But the people of Israel became afraid and they made an awful decision. They told Moses that they didn't want to go into God's presence—they were too afraid. "So you go talk to the Lord, Moses, and then come tell us what He says. But we're going to worship God from far away." Then the Bible tells us that "the people stood far away, but Moses came near."

As Don read this story, he found himself coming to a decision in his heart. "I don't want to worship God from far away," he thought. "I want to be like Moses!" He realized that seeking the Lord was a choice, and that no matter how hard it was to be where the Lord was (even if there was thunder and lightning!), he was choosing to get as close to God as he could. He found the same desire in his heart that had been there when he was a little boy and underlined that verse in Psalm 27.

In the same Psalm, we read another verse that says, "When You, Lord, said, 'Seek My face,' my heart said to You, 'Your face, Lord, I will seek'" (v. 8). We can make that choice any time. Don was all grown up when he wrote the song, but he was just a boy when the desire to be near God started in his heart. You don't have to be grown up to be where God is. He wants you to come near right now!

I Want to Be Where You Are

DM

Don Moen

I just want to be where___ You are,___

dwell- ing dai - ly in___ Your pres - ence;___ I don't want to

wor- ship from___ a - far,___ draw me near___ to where___ You are.___

I want to be where

You are,___ dwell- ing in Your pres- ence,___ feast- ing at Your

ta - ble,___ sur- round- ed by Your glo - ry;___ In Your

pres- ence,___ that's___ where I al - ways want___ to___ be,___

I just want___ to be,___ I just want___ to be___ with You.___

© 1989 by Integrity's Hosanna! Music, P.O. Box 851622, Mobile, AL 36685-1622.
All rights reserved. Used by permission.

Every day I pray for my children. One thing that I ask the Lord to do is make my children's hearts bigger so that they can love Him more. The Lord has done that and is continuing to do that! They all asked Jesus into their lives when they were young and they all love Him and obey Him.

There is something very exciting about asking Jesus into your life when you are young! You get to do something most people don't—you get to serve and obey Jesus for your *entire* life. That is what happened with the author of the song, "My Jesus, I Love Thee." William Featherstone came to know the Lord when he was sixteen years old and he wrote this song while he was still a teenager! Each verse tells us something about how William planned to show His love for the Lord. Verse 1 tells us that William was going to love the Lord by living purely, while verse 2 gives praise for our salvation through Jesus. In verses 3 and 4, William talks about how he will love the Lord his whole life and even after he dies and goes to heaven.

The Bible has something to say about how we are supposed to love the Lord too. Jesus says, "You shall love the Lord your God will all your heart, with all your soul, with all your mind, and with all your strength" (Mark 12:30). That's four ways we can show our love to the Lord! But what do they all mean?

"*With all your heart*" is talking about our emotions—the things we care about, the things we feel. Loving the Lord with all of your heart means that you choose not only to love Him, but to love the things He loves: things like kindness, joy, self-control, and peace. It also means that when you feel angry or impatient or mean that you ask the Lord to help you get rid of that feeling and be the kind of person He wants you to be.

"*With all your soul*" is the part of you that accepts God's gift of salvation. Loving the Lord with this part of ourselves means that we let the Lord make us completely new on the inside. For example if you have a hard time obeying your parents, the Lord wants to help you become new in that part of your life so that you'll *want* to obey.

"*With all your mind*" means that you think about the same things God thinks about. David wrote, "Let the things I think about be acceptable to You, Lord" (Ps. 19:14). Then Paul writes about the things that we *should* be thinking about: things that are true, moral, right and fair, pure, beautiful, honorable and respectful, excellent, and worth praise (Phil. 4:8).

"*With all your strength*" is talking about loving the Lord with our physical bodies—the things we do. You aren't loving the Lord with your body if you're punching your brother or saying mean things to your sister. We are not just to *say* that we love one another (or the Lord), but we are also to show it by our actions (1 John 3:18).

Is there a place in your life where you need to love Jesus more? Ask Him to make your heart bigger so that you can love Him more . . . and He'll do it!

My Jesus I Love Thee

William R. Featherstone
Adoniram J. Gordon
1. My Je - sus, I love Thee, I know Thou art mine; For
2. I love Thee, be - cause Thou hast first lov - ed me, And
3. I'll love Thee in life, I will love Thee in death, And
4. In man - sions of glo - ry and end - less de - light, I'll
Thee all the fol - lies of sin I re - sign; My
pur - chased my par - don on Cal - va - ry's tree; I
praise Thee as long as Thou lend - est me breath; And
ev - er a - dore Thee in heav - en so bright; I'll
gra - cious Re - deem - er, my Sav - ior art Thou; If
love Thee for wear - ing the thorns on Thy brow; If
say when the death - dew lies cold on my brow; If
sing with the glit - ter - ing crown on my brow; If
ev - er I loved Thee, my Je - sus, 'tis now.
ev - er I loved Thee, my Je - sus, 'tis now.
ev - er I loved Thee, my Je - sus, 'tis now.
ev - er I loved Thee, my Je - sus, 'tis now. A - men.

Did you know that the Bible talks about different kinds of love? In our language, we use the same word, "love," for all the different kinds of love, but in the language that the New Testament was first written (Greek), it uses three different words!

The first word describes the kind of love you have for your friends and family. It's the warm and trusting kind of love you feel for your mom and dad. It's the affection you feel for your best friend at school. It could even describe the respect you have for your pastor, teacher, or doctor. It's the kind of love you feel for people most often.

The second word for love describes the special kind of love that you will someday have for the person you marry. That may not sound very interesting to you right now, but the Lord has a special and specific person to be your partner when you grow up. You can even begin praying for him or her *right now* that the Lord will cause that person to grow up loving Him too.

The third word describes God's love. This kind of love is the best kind of love because it comes into our lives through a miracle. We are filled with God's love only when we ask Jesus to come into our hearts and live in our lives. That's a miracle! God's love also fills us so that we can love people who are unlovable. That's a miracle too. Jesus said, "If you only love the people who love you, how is that different from anybody else? Even ungodly people do that!" (Matt. 5:46) Instead, Jesus calls us to love our enemies (v. 44). Only when Jesus lives in our hearts can that kind of selfless love happen in us. That's why godly (or divine) love is the best—it's miraculous.

"Love Divine, All Loves Excelling" is a song written by Charles Wesley to describe how awesome God's love is. Although the language of the song is a little old-fashioned, if you read carefully you'll find out lots of things about God's love. Read and see if you can find where Charles refers to these things about God's love and then look up the verses and read where the Bible says the same things.

God's love is the best (1 Cor. 13:13). Love sent Jesus to earth (John 3:16 and 1 John 3:16). Jesus is compassionate (loving, merciful, and understanding) (Mark 6:34). God fills us with the Spirit (Gal. 5:22). God's love provides us with an inheritance (1 Peter 1:3-4). God gives rest to those He loves (Zeph. 3:17). God's love purifies us (1 John 3:2-3). God completes what He starts (Phil. 1:6). God delivers us (2 Cor. 1:10; Col. 1:13). God's love is perfect (1 John 2:5; 4:12). We are constantly being made more like Jesus (Phil. 1:9; 2 Cor. 3:18).

Love Divine, All Loves Excelling

Charles Wesley
John Zundel
1. Love di-vine, all loves ex-cel-ling, Joy of heaven, to earth come down;
2. Breathe, O breathe Thy lov-ing Spir-it In-to ev-ery trou-bled breast;
3. Come, Al-might-y to de-liv-er, Let us all Thy life re-ceive;
4. Fin-ish then Thy new cre-a-tion, Pure and spot-less let us be;
Fix in us Thy hum-ble dwell-ing, All Thy faith-ful mer-cies crown:
Let us all in Thee in-her-it, Let us find the prom-ised rest;
Sud-den-ly re-turn, and nev-er, Nev-er-more Thy tem-ples leave.
Let us see Thy great sal-va-tion, Per-fect-ly re-stored in Thee;
Je-sus, Thou art all com-pas-sion, Pure, un-bound-ed love Thou art;
Take a-way the love of sin-ning, Al-pha and O-me-ga be;
Thee we would be al-ways bless-ing, Serve Thee as Thy hosts a-bove,
Changed from glo-ry in-to glo-ry, Till in heaven we take our place,
Vis-it us with Thy sal-va-tion, En-ter ev-ery trem-bling heart.
End of faith, as its be-gin-ning, Set our hearts at lib-er-ty.
Pray, and praise Thee with-out ceas-ing, Glo-ry in Thy per-fect love.
Till we cast our crowns be-fore Thee, Lost in won-der, love, and praise!

March: Easter

I've always loved the story of what happened on Palm Sunday! It's happy! It's exciting! It's filled with joy! In my imagination, I can feel the hustle and bustle of the crowd. I can imagine the dust in the air and see children climbing trees to pull down branches to wave in celebration. And I can hear the praises of the people as Jesus rides into town. In fact, I have even walked on the very path Jesus took that day. I suppose it must have looked a little different 2,000 years ago—but I can imagine how it must have been!

When we read the story of Palm Sunday in Luke, we read about the group of people who welcomed Jesus (19:37-38). It says that as Jesus came into Jerusalem on the donkey, a large crowd of disciples began to "*rejoice* and *praise* God for all the mighty works they had seen." They welcomed Jesus by allowing *joy* to fill their hearts and *praise* to come from their mouths! From their example, we can see how our praise welcomes the Lord, and having Him with us is one of the greatest things about knowing Him! In fact, the Lord promises us that He will never leave us or abandon us (Heb. 13:5).

But did you know what God's presence *does* for us? Where God's presence is, there is perfect joy! (Ps. 16:11) That's something that the Lord wants to give to every one of us—joy! The Bible teaches us that once Jesus lives in our hearts, the "fruit of the Spirit" begin to grow there, and one of those fruit is joy (Gal. 5:22). So just like you carefully water a plant, you need to let joy grow in your heart. Then the Prophet Isaiah wrote that the Lord wants to give us joy instead of sadness (61:3). Is there something in your life that you're sad about? Share it with the Lord and leave it with Him. Find your joy in Him. He will take care of everything else. The Psalms also tell us that our joy is supposed to be based in our salvation—now *that's* something to be joyful about! (95:1-2; see also Hab. 3:18) Our sins are forgiven and we will live with the Lord forever!

Did you know, though, that being joyful is a choice? There was another group of people who were on the road on Palm Sunday (Luke 19:39-40). It says that these people were upset and told Jesus to stop His disciples from praising. These people not only didn't believe that God sent Jesus, they didn't want anyone else to believe. They didn't want to praise, so they tried to stop everyone else from praising. Like those people, you can resist or fight against joy if you want to. But a better idea is to be like the first group of people! Choose to be filled with joy and praise the Lord!

Welcome God's presence today. Let Him fill your heart with His joy. And when you do, you'll find that joy beginning to overflow your heart with songs of praise!

Joyful, Joyful We Adore Thee

Henry Van Dyke
Arr. from Ludwig von Beethoven
1. Joy - ful, joy - ful, we a - dore Thee, God of glor - ry, Lord of love;
2. All Thy works with joy sur-round Thee, Earth and heav'n re - flect Thy rays,
3. Thou art giv - ing and for - giv - ing, Ev - er bless - ing, ev - er blest,
4. Mor-tals join the might - y cho - rus Which the morn-ing stars be - gan;
Hearts un - fold like flow'rs be - fore Thee, Hail Thee as the sun a - bove.
Stars and an - gels sing a - round Thee, Cen - ter of un - bro - ken praise;
Well-spring of the joy of liv - ing, O - cean depth of hap - py rest!
Fa - ther love is reign - ing o'er us, Broth - er love binds man to man.
Melt the clouds of sin and sad - ness; Drive the dark of doubt a - way;
Field and for - est, vale and moun-tain, Bloss -'ming mead-ow, flash-ing sea,
Thou our Fa - ther, Christ our Broth - er, All who live in love are Thine;
Ev - er singing, march we on - ward, Vic - tors in the midst of strife;
Giv - er of im - mor - tal glad-ness, Fill us with the light of day!
Chant-ing bird and flow-ing foun-tain, Call us to re - joice in Thee.
Teach us how to love each oth - er, Lift us to the Joy Di - vine.
Joy - ful mu - sic lifts us sun-ward In the tri-umph song of life.

Do you like mysteries? When I was a little girl I liked reading detective stories and finding out how the mystery would be solved. Maybe you like to read mysteries too. Or maybe you like to play games like Clue, because a good mystery can be a lot of fun.

Did you know that God likes a good mystery? In the song, "And Can It Be That I Should Gain," Charles Wesley writes about the mystery that God likes: the mystery of Jesus coming to earth to die for our sins. The best thing about this mystery is that we don't have to wait to find out how it is solved because the Bible tells us the whole story!

When God created the world, He made it perfect, sinless, and filled with beauty. Then He created Adam and Eve to be in charge of and take care of this wonderful place He had made. But Adam and Eve failed and disobeyed God. By doing this, they brought sin into God's perfect creation. The punishment for sin is death; so Adam's and Eve's sin also brought death into the world, and in the process, the devil tricked them into turning over the responsibility of running the earth to him. Here is where the mystery comes in: there needed to be a way to undo what people's sin and the devil's deceit had done. But how could this take place?

Well, God loved us so much that He came up with a plan. There needed to be Someone who could live a sinless, perfect life to take the punishment for us. If they were sinless, they wouldn't be dying for their own sins, but could truly take the place of another person. God knew that no human being would ever be able to do that, so He decided that He Himself, in Jesus, would come to earth as a man and die for our sins. That way if *any person* would believe in what God had provided for us, he or she would be able to (1) come back into fellowship with God by having their sins forgiven; (2) defeat the devil who was now ruling things; and (3) step back into being in charge of what God had given them.

It was an incredible plan! First, that God would take our place of punishment for the wrong we had done! Then second, that He wanted a way to give back everything He had originally planned for us! So this song declares: "'Tis mystery all! The immortal dies! Who can explore His strange design?" In our words today, Charles was saying, "What a mystery! God died in *my* place! Who can ever fully understand God's incredible plan!" The Bible says, "The mystery which had been hidden for many centuries and from many peoples has now been revealed to us—those who God has made holy through Jesus Christ" (Col. 1:26).

This *is* the best mystery! Not only do we know how everything comes out, but we get to be a part of it by asking Jesus into our hearts! Have you ever done that? If you have, you're just beginning to learn how wonderful it is to have Jesus live in your life, to be forgiven, and to be able to talk to Him as a friend. If you haven't, why don't you ask Jesus into your heart now? He loves you so much and He's provided a wonderful plan so that you too can know, walk, and talk with God!

God so loved the world that He gave...

And Can It Be That I Should Gain

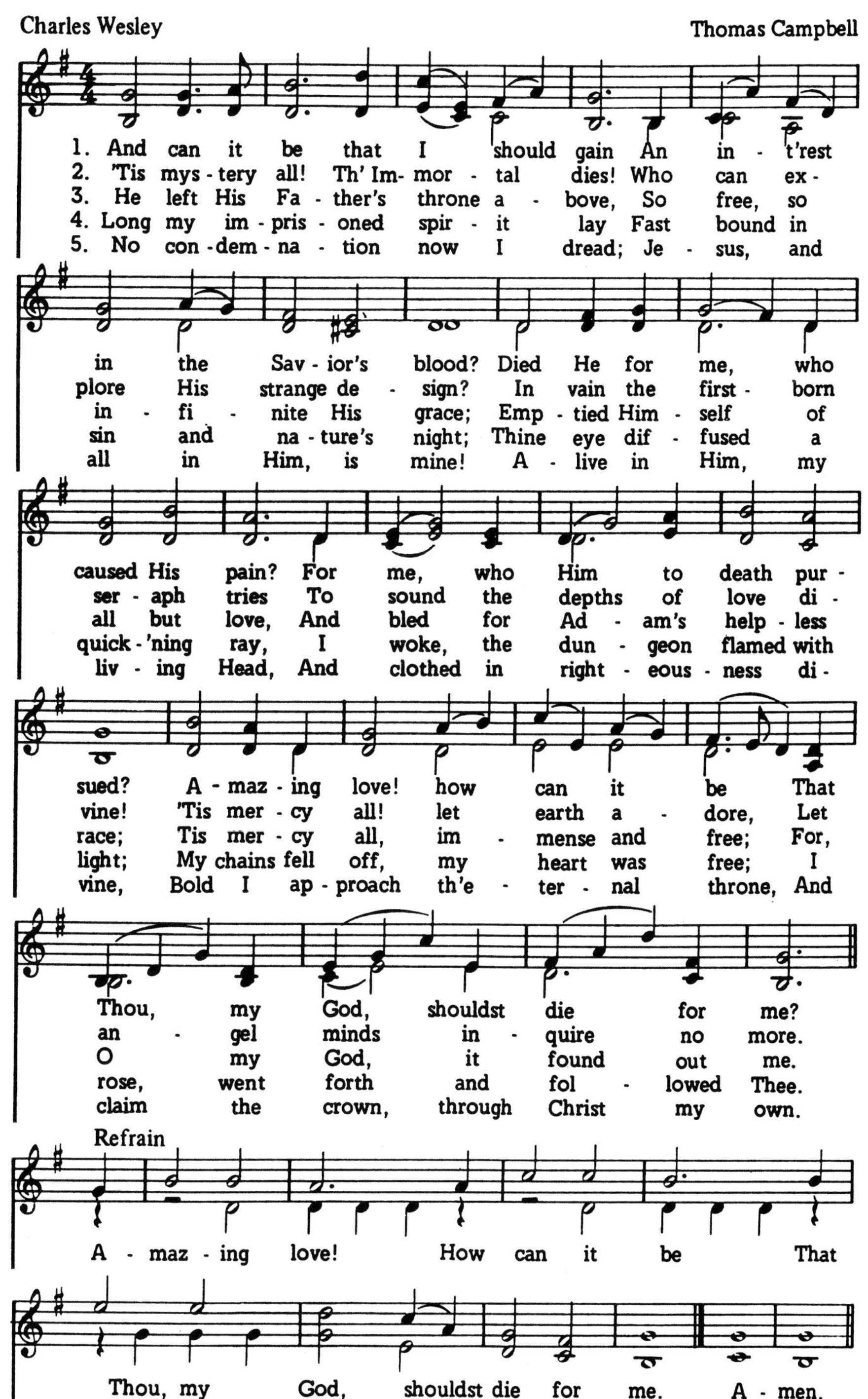

Charles Wesley
Thomas Campbell
1. And can it be that I should gain An in - t'rest
2. 'Tis mys - tery all! Th' Im - mor - tal dies! Who can ex -
3. He left His Fa - ther's throne a - bove, So free, so
4. Long my im - pris - oned spir - it lay Fast bound in
5. No con - dem - na - tion now I dread; Je - sus, and
in the Sav - ior's blood? Died He for me, who
plore His strange de - sign? In vain the first - born
in - fi - nite His grace; Emp - tied Him - self of
sin and na - ture's night; Thine eye dif - fused a
all in Him, is mine! A - live in Him, my
caused His pain? For me, who Him to death pur -
ser - aph tries To sound the depths of love di -
all but love, And bled for Ad - am's help - less
quick - 'ning ray, I woke, the dun - geon flamed with
liv - ing Head, And clothed in right - eous - ness di -
sued? A - maz - ing love! how can it be That
vine! 'Tis mer - cy all! let earth a - dore, Let
race; Tis mer - cy all, im - mense and free; For,
light; My chains fell off, my heart was free; I
vine, Bold I ap - proach th'e - ter - nal throne, And
Thou, my God, shouldst die for me?
an - gel minds in - quire no more.
O my God, it found out me.
rose, went forth and fol - lowed Thee.
claim the crown, through Christ my own.
Refrain
A - maz - ing love! How can it be That
Thou, my God, shouldst die for me. A - men.

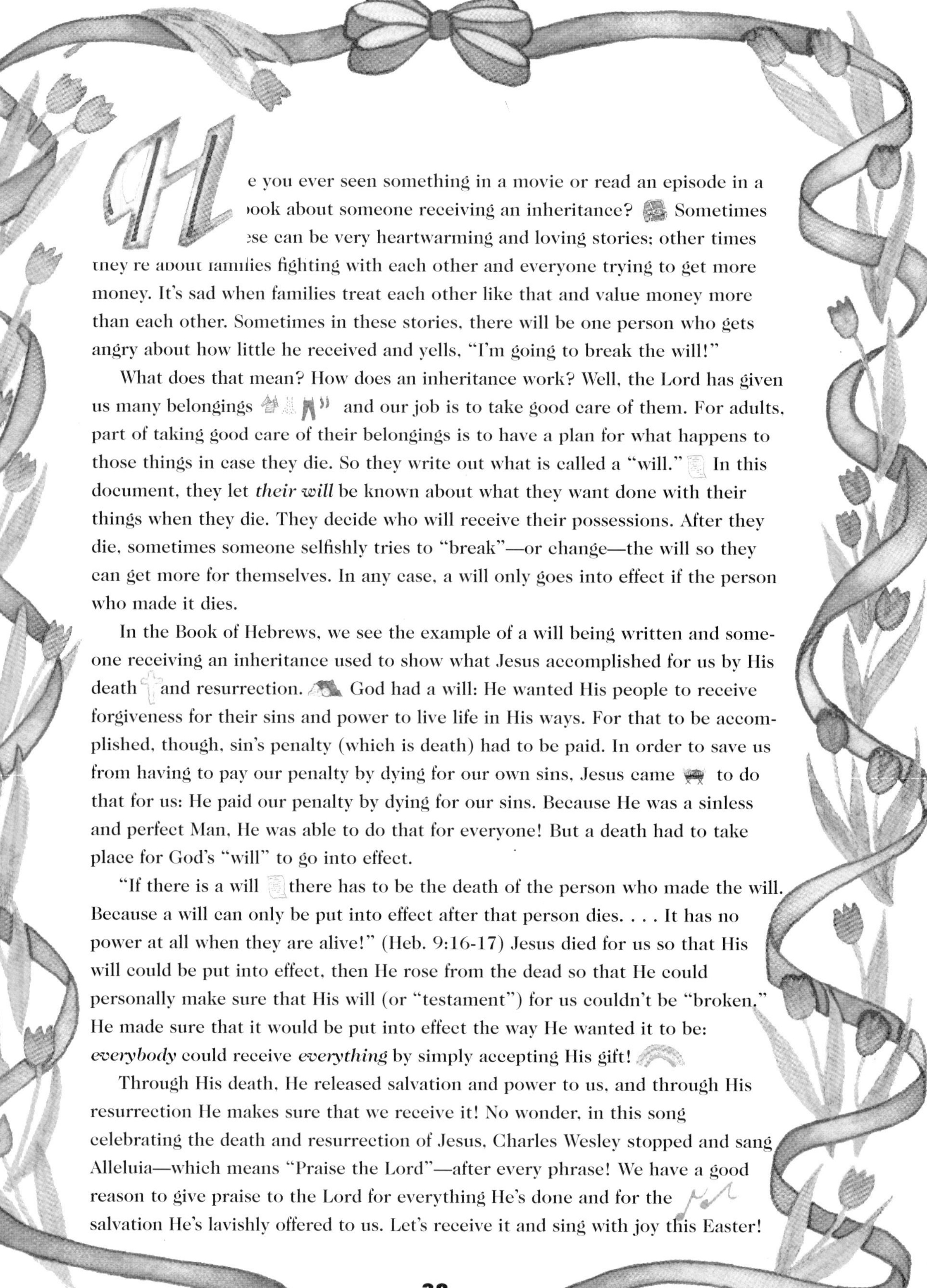

Have you ever seen something in a movie or read an episode in a book about someone receiving an inheritance? Sometimes these can be very heartwarming and loving stories; other times they're about families fighting with each other and everyone trying to get more money. It's sad when families treat each other like that and value money more than each other. Sometimes in these stories, there will be one person who gets angry about how little he received and yells, "I'm going to break the will!"

What does that mean? How does an inheritance work? Well, the Lord has given us many belongings and our job is to take good care of them. For adults, part of taking good care of their belongings is to have a plan for what happens to those things in case they die. So they write out what is called a "will." In this document, they let *their will* be known about what they want done with their things when they die. They decide who will receive their possessions. After they die, sometimes someone selfishly tries to "break"—or change—the will so they can get more for themselves. In any case, a will only goes into effect if the person who made it dies.

In the Book of Hebrews, we see the example of a will being written and someone receiving an inheritance used to show what Jesus accomplished for us by His death and resurrection. God had a will: He wanted His people to receive forgiveness for their sins and power to live life in His ways. For that to be accomplished, though, sin's penalty (which is death) had to be paid. In order to save us from having to pay our penalty by dying for our own sins, Jesus came to do that for us: He paid our penalty by dying for our sins. Because He was a sinless and perfect Man, He was able to do that for everyone! But a death had to take place for God's "will" to go into effect.

"If there is a will there has to be the death of the person who made the will. Because a will can only be put into effect after that person dies. . . . It has no power at all when they are alive!" (Heb. 9:16-17) Jesus died for us so that His will could be put into effect, then He rose from the dead so that He could personally make sure that His will (or "testament") for us couldn't be "broken." He made sure that it would be put into effect the way He wanted it to be: *everybody* could receive *everything* by simply accepting His gift!

Through His death, He released salvation and power to us, and through His resurrection He makes sure that we receive it! No wonder, in this song celebrating the death and resurrection of Jesus, Charles Wesley stopped and sang Alleluia—which means "Praise the Lord"—after every phrase! We have a good reason to give praise to the Lord for everything He's done and for the salvation He's lavishly offered to us. Let's receive it and sing with joy this Easter!

Christ the Lord Is Risen Today

Charles Wesley
From "Lyra Davidica"
1. Christ the Lord is risen to - day, Al - - le - lu - ia!
2. Lives a - gain our glo - rious King, Al - - le - lu - ia!
3. Love's re - deem - ing work is done, Al - - le - lu - ia!
4. Soar we now where Christ has led, Al - - le - lu - ia!
Sons of men and an - gels say, Al - - le - lu - ia!
Where, O Death, is now thy sting? Al - - le - lu - ia!
Fought the fight, the bat - tle won, Al - - le - lu - ia!
Fol - lowing our ex - alt - ed Head, Al - - le - lu - ia!
Raise your joys and tri - umphs high, Al - - le - lu - ia!
Dy - ing once He all doth save, Al - - le - lu - ia!
Death in vain for - bids Him rise, Al - - le - lu - ia!
Made like Him, like Him we rise, Al - - le - lu - ia!
Sing, ye heavens, and earth, re - ply, Al - - le - lu - ia!
Where thy vic - to - ry, O Grave? Al - - le - lu - ia!
Christ hath o - pened par - a - dise, Al - - le - lu - ia!
Ours the cross, the grave, the skies, Al - - le - lu - ia!

Crowns are beautiful! Have you ever seen a picture of a real crown? They are covered with gold and decorated with beautiful jewels. I remember seeing drawings of gorgeous crowns in fairy tale books, and I always wanted one of my own! I even used to have pretend crowns I would wear! But have you ever thought about what a crown represents? It's a symbol of rulership and all of the responsibilities that go along with being a ruler. It represents the responsibility of running a kingdom skillfully and productively. It means that when your kingdom is attacked, you will protect and fight for the people who are under your rule. Wearing a crown can also show that you have conquered someone who has invaded your territory.

Long ago when one king conquered another, the king who had won the battle would take the crown of the defeated king and wear it himself. We can see this described in the life of King David. The Bible says that after a battle, the crown of the conquered king was placed on David's head (2 Sam. 12:30). In doing this, David was saying to the people in the conquered kingdom that he was their new king.

In the Book of Revelation, Jesus is described as having many crowns on His head (Rev. 19:11-12). What does this say about Jesus? First it says that He rules over a lot, and the Bible talks about some of His crowns. The first crown it describes Jesus wearing is a crown of thorns (Matt. 27:29; Mark 15:17; John 19:2). He wore that crown to accomplish our salvation. Later, Jesus is described as wearing a golden crown, (Rev. 14:14) and He is "crowned with glory and honor" (Heb. 2:9).

Jesus being "crowned with many crowns" has a second meaning, though. It means He is a conqueror. When He was here on earth, He said that the reason He came was to "preach deliverance to the captives" (Luke 4:18). He came to set us free! But to do that, He had to conquer what was holding us prisoner. In His death and resurrection, Jesus "led captivity captive" (Eph. 4:8). Anything that can hold us captive in our spirits, souls, or bodies—Jesus conquered! And He's still doing it! The Bible says that Jesus "went forth conquering and to conquer" (Rev. 6:2). All the things in the Book of Revelation haven't happened yet, so this verse tells us that Jesus' "conquering days" aren't over! He still can and will conquer the things that hold us captive in our spirits.

Maybe in your life, the thing that holds you captive is anger or pride or disobedience. Jesus can conquer that and then He will rule over that part of your life instead of it ruling over you. What area of your life needs Jesus' rule? We can invite His rule into our lives every day. Try it and see how His conquering power helps you conquer things in your life!

Crown Him with Many Crowns

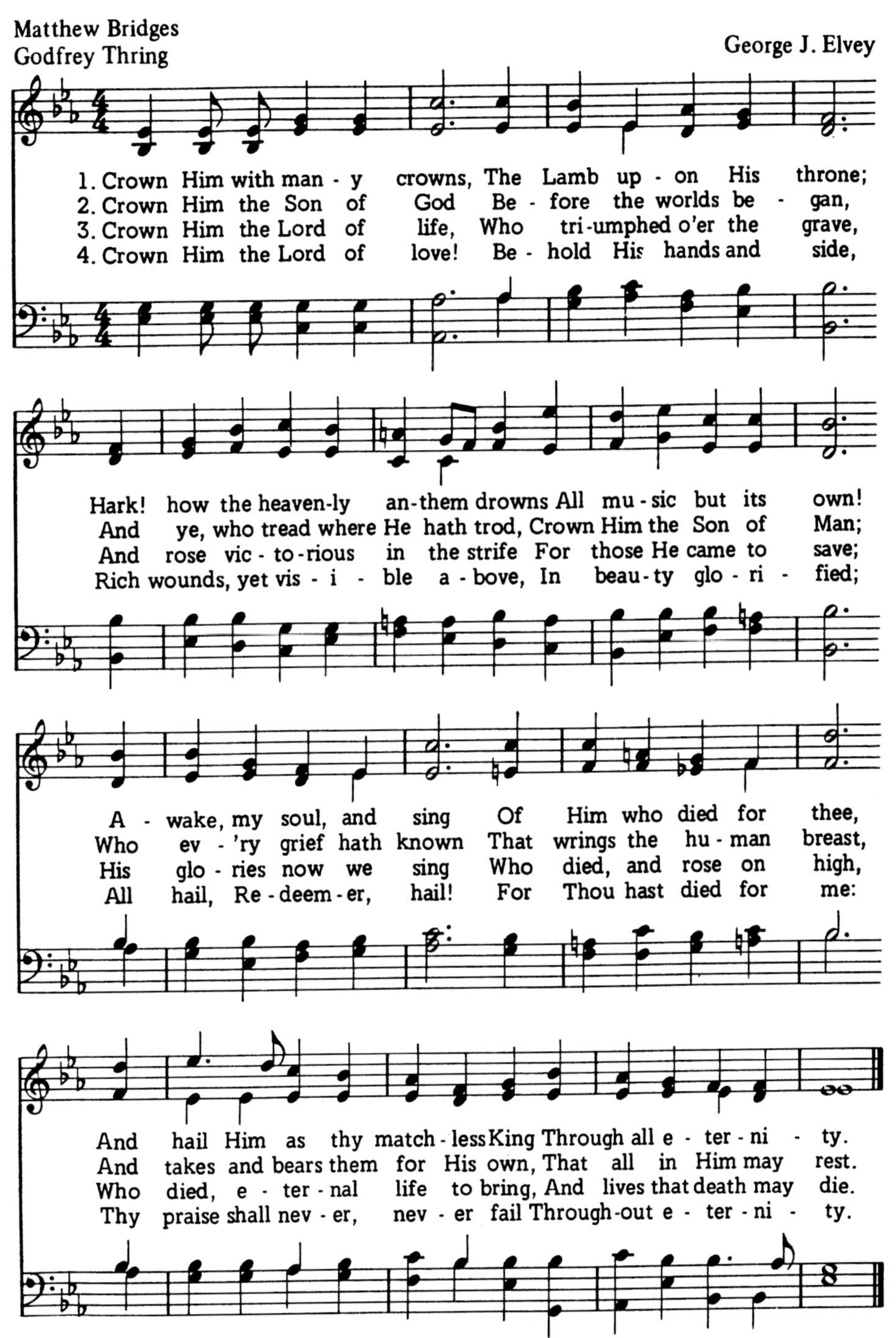
Matthew Bridges
Godfrey Thring
George J. Elvey
1. Crown Him with man - y crowns, The Lamb up - on His throne;
2. Crown Him the Son of God Be - fore the worlds be - gan,
3. Crown Him the Lord of life, Who tri-umphed o'er the grave,
4. Crown Him the Lord of love! Be - hold His hands and side,
Hark! how the heaven-ly an-them drowns All mu - sic but its own!
And ye, who tread where He hath trod, Crown Him the Son of Man;
And rose vic - to - rious in the strife For those He came to save;
Rich wounds, yet vis - i - ble a - bove, In beau - ty glo - ri - fied;
A - wake, my soul, and sing Of Him who died for thee,
Who ev - 'ry grief hath known That wrings the hu - man breast,
His glo - ries now we sing Who died, and rose on high,
All hail, Re - deem - er, hail! For Thou hast died for me:
And hail Him as thy match - less King Through all e - ter - ni - ty.
And takes and bears them for His own, That all in Him may rest.
Who died, e - ter - nal life to bring, And lives that death may die.
Thy praise shall nev - er, nev - er fail Through-out e - ter - ni - ty.

I asked Jesus into my heart when I was just a little girl—seven years old—and I've served and loved Jesus my whole life. But it took a long time for me to truly understand that I was a sinner. Being so young when I received Jesus, I hadn't ever really done anything so awful, and I guess I didn't think I was all that bad. One day, however, I suddenly realized that it only takes *one* sin to make someone a sinner. I knew I had lied at least once. I knew I had disobeyed my parents at least once. I knew I had slugged my brother at least once. And now I also knew that—yes—I was a sinner.

That helped me understand better what Jesus did on the cross for me. "What you earn when you sin is death" (Rom. 6:23), so if I were a sinner (and I was), the penalty for that, according to the Bible, was death. But Jesus chose to become my Redeemer and accept that punishment of death in my place! (Just like if someone took my place and got a spanking when it was really *me* who had done something wrong.)

"Redeemer" is not a word that is used very much anymore, but to understand what Jesus did, it's an important word for us to know. The dictionary gives several definitions for "redeemer," and all of them can help us understand this word.

First it means *to buy back something that belongs to you* or *to set free by paying a ransom.* God created us, so we all belonged to Him. But through Adam and Eve, the devil stole us all away. Jesus paid the price, the ransom, for us with His own life when He shed His blood on the cross.

Second, "redeem" means *to turn in a coupon for a prize.* Just think! Jesus turned *Himself* in so that He could receive a prize. That prize was us! The fact that He was willing to do that shows how valuable He thinks we are.

Then, the dictionary listed a synonym for redeem: *rescue.* Jesus rescued us from someone whose only goal was to steal, kill, and destroy us (John 10:10). The Psalms also tell us that the Lord has redeemed us from the enemy! (107:1-2)

That's what this song invites us to do: give our Redeemer thanks. As you do, look at these other reasons the Bible gives us to praise our Redeemer. "Lord, You have defended my soul in heaven's court; You have redeemed my life" (Lam. 3:58). "We've been given a completely right standing through the redemption that is in Christ Jesus" (Rom. 3:24). "Christ has redeemed us from the curse" (Gal. 3:13) and through that redemption we have "forgiveness of sins" (Eph. 1:7). And our redemption is eternal! (Heb. 9:12)

Sing, O sing of my Redeemer!

I Will Sing of My Redeemer

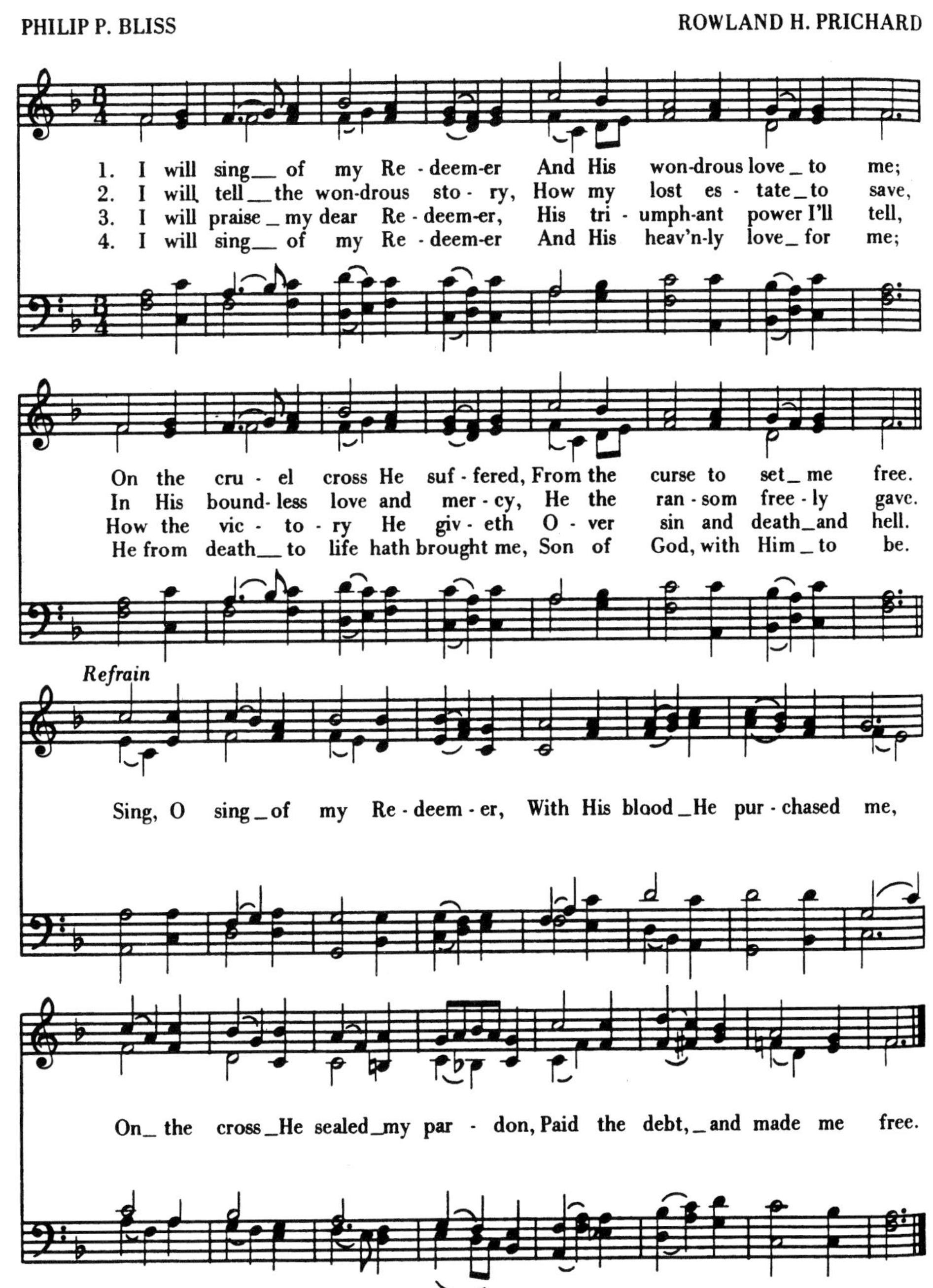
PHILIP P. BLISS
ROWLAND H. PRICHARD
1. I will sing of my Re-deem-er And His won-drous love to me;
2. I will tell the won-drous sto-ry, How my lost es-tate to save,
3. I will praise my dear Re-deem-er, His tri-umph-ant power I'll tell,
4. I will sing of my Re-deem-er And His heav'n-ly love for me;
On the cru-el cross He suf-fered, From the curse to set me free.
In His bound-less love and mer-cy, He the ran-som free-ly gave.
How the vic-to-ry He giv-eth O-ver sin and death and hell.
He from death to life hath brought me, Son of God, with Him to be.
Refrain
Sing, O sing of my Re-deem-er, With His blood He pur-chased me,
On the cross He sealed my par-don, Paid the debt, and made me free.

April: Jesus' Name

Have you ever seen a picture of the Queen of England? Maybe you've seen her on the news. If you have, you've noticed that every person who comes up to her bows or curtsies before they speak to her. By doing this, they acknowledge that her position of rulership is higher than theirs. It's a sign of respect and shows that they recognize that the Queen represents the power of an entire nation.

It's the same way when we come to Jesus to worship Him: we are acknowledging His rulership and His position as leader over us. We're saying that we recognize His power—the power that has conquered Satan and death, the power that raised Him from the dead, and the power that brings us new life. The difference is that people aren't worshiping the Queen, but we *are* worshiping Jesus.

What exactly does worship mean then? Is it respectful? Of course. Does it pay honor to the person? Yes. But there are several other ideas behind worship that make it more than just honoring someone.

First, worship is acknowledging the Lord as God. Many people worship things other than God, and when they do they are acknowledging that whatever *they* worship is *their* god. Some people worship money. Some people worship success. Some people worship being liked by everyone. They may not physically bow down to it, but they've made it the most important thing in their lives and everything they do centers around that thing. When we worship the Lord, we are saying that He is our God and that our lives center around Him.

The second thing we do in worship is to place value on the One we are worshiping. When we worship the Lord, we are saying, "Not only are You my Lord and my God, but You are worth . . . *everything*! Because of that, I owe You everything."

Finally, our worship expresses love. I'm sure that not everyone who bows to the Queen loves her. But when we bow to the Lord, it is a way of expressing our love for Him. In the Book of 1 John, the apostle wrote, "We love Him because He first loved us" (1 John 4:19). Later, he also wrote in praise, "To Him who loved us and washed us from our sins . . . to Him be glory and dominion forever" (Rev. 1:5-6).

"All Hail the Power of Jesus' Name" is a song that calls us to that kind of loving worship and acknowledgment of Jesus' place of ruling in our lives. The last verse of the song says, "O that with yonder sacred throng we at His feet may fall!" That's a rather fancy way of saying, when we're with those who love the Lord (sacred throng), let us all bow in worship. There is *no* better way to tell the Lord that we love Him than by praising Him. Let's do that today!

All Hail the Power of Jesus' Name

Edward Perronet
Alt. by John Rippon
Oliver Holden
1. All hail the pow'r of Je - sus' name! Let an - gels pros - trate fall; Bring forth the roy - al di - a - dem, And crown Him Lord of all; Bring forth the roy - al di - a - dem, And crown Him Lord of all!
2. Ye cho - sen seed of Is - rael's race, Ye ran - somed from the fall, Hail Him who saves you by His grace, And crown Him Lord of all; Hail Him who saves you by His grace, And crown Him Lord of all!
3. Let ev - 'ry kin - dred, ev - 'ry tribe, On this ter - res - trial ball, To Him all maj - es - ty as - cribe, And crown Him Lord of all; To Him all maj - es - ty as - scribe, And crown Him Lord of all!
4. O that with yon - der sa - cred throng We at His feet may fall! We'll join the ev - er - last - ing song, And crown Him Lord of all; We'll join the ev - er - last - ing song, And crown Him Lord of all!

Nothing is greater than Jesus' name! The Bible says that "at the name of Jesus every knee will bow . . . and that every tongue should confess that Jesus Christ is Lord" (Phil. 2:10-11). When Jesus sent His disciples out to preach, He sent them in the power of His name (Mark 16:17). To help understand the power Jesus was giving us in His name, the Bible gives many names for Jesus—kind of like nicknames. Look at all these names for Jesus and what they teach us about Him. Take time to look up all the verses too! He is called:

ALMIGHTY—because there is nothing greater than Jesus (Gen. 17:1; Rev. 11:17).

THE BREAD OF LIFE—because He takes away the emptiness in our lives and fills us with Himself (John 6:33-35).

THE DOOR —because He's the only way to God (John 10:7-9; 14:6).

THE LAMB OF GOD—because He became the sacrifice for our sins (Lev. 4:32-35; John 1:29; 1 Peter 1:19; Rev. 5:12).

THE ROCK—because He's steady and unchanging (Ps. 18:2; 1 Cor. 10:4; James 1:17).

THE WORD—because Jesus is a physical picture of God's spoken promises (John 1:1, 14).

THE GOOD SHEPHERD —because just like a shepherd leads his sheep, Jesus leads us (Ps. 23; John 10:11).

THE RESURRECTION AND THE LIFE—because we receive new life from Him (John 11:25).

PRINCE OF PEACE —because wherever Jesus is, there will be peace (Isa. 9:6; 1 Cor. 14:33; Eph. 2:14).

COUNSELOR—because He helps us understand His Word and ourselves, and teaches us what to do (Isa. 9:6; John 16:13; 1 Cor. 14:25).

EXCELLENT—because everything He does is done well (Ps. 8:1; Heb. 1:4).

THE BEGINNING AND THE END—because He sees how everything will turn out (Isa. 46:9-10; Phil. 1:6; Rev. 1:8).

IMMANUEL —because He's always with us. Immanuel actually means "God with us" (Isa. 7:14; Matt. 1:23).

SAVIOR—He has saved us from sin and the penalty it brings (John 4:42; Acts 5:31; 1 Tim. 4:10; Jude 25).

Jesus' Name Almighty

Translated from Danish
by JACK HAYFORD
DAVID WELANDER
1. Je - sus' Name all might- y in pow - er change - less al -
2. Sound of free-dom, ring - ing with beau - ty, sing Je - sus'
3. Je - sus' Name shines in -to the dark - ness bea - con - ing
though ___ the ag - es roll. Je - sus' Name no force can an -
Name ___ through all the earth. None like this can bring hope or
hope ___ where all is gloom. Pain and cha - os seem to be
nul its pow - er to heal ___ the hu - man soul. Like the
com - fort Je - sus the name ___ of match - less worth. When we
win - ning Je - sus the name ___ that sounds their doom. When all
bloom ___ of life in spring-time, comes its mes - sage to all
speak ___ the Name of Je - sus, hell and hat - tred have to
time ___ shall reach its end - ing, and the sun ___ shall shine no
men. Je - sus' Name is wor - thy of glo - ry. Let us ex -
flee. By that name the king - dom of heav - en length - ens the
more. Je - sus' Name shall theme all the prais - es of the re -
alt ___ His Name a - gain.
bounds _ of vic - to - ry. How I love __ the Name of Je - sus. It has
deemed _ on heav - en's shore.
set ___ my soul a - flame. None like this in earth or in
heav - en match - less the power ___ of Je - sus' Name.

The Bible says that there is salvation in no other name than Jesus' name (Acts 4:12). Have you ever thought about how great that is? Through Jesus we have forgiveness of sins, a promise of spending forever with the Lord in heaven, and we become part of God's family! The Bible even tells us that the Lord removes our sins so that it is as though they never happened! Sometimes I think that's the greatest miracle . . . that the Lord *forgets* our sins! I've always thought that proves how great He is . . . I mean, have you ever tried to forget something on purpose? I have. And it seems like the more I try to forget it the more I think about it! Yet God is so powerful, He can pick and choose what He will forget . . . and He chooses to forget our sins the instant we ask for forgiveness. All of that happens through the power of Jesus' name!

But that isn't all that the Lord promises us through salvation. In Acts 3, we see something else that the Lord wants to do for us: He wants to heal our bodies.

One day Peter and John were going to the temple in Jerusalem to worship the Lord. As they were walking in, they saw a crippled beggar sitting by the entrance asking for money. Peter and John turned to the man and said, "We don't have any money. But what we do have, we're giving to you: in Jesus' name, get up and walk!" Immediately the man was healed and could walk! And that happened through the power of Jesus' name!

Later, we read in Acts 4, that Peter and John were arrested for healing the man. When they were asked how this man was healed, Peter linked the power of Jesus to heal *and* forgive and boldly said,

> *Let it be known to you all, and to all the people of Israel, that by the name of Jesus Christ of Nazareth . . . this man stands here before you whole. Nor is there salvation in any other, for there is no other name under heaven given among men by which we must be saved (Acts 4:10, 12, NKJV).*

In Matthew 14:36, the Gospel writer used a word to describe how Jesus brought forgiveness and healing to people. Because Matthew wrote in another language, it sounds like a funny word to us: *diasozo* (dee-ah-sewed-zo). But even if it sounds funny, it's an important word because it means several things at once: it can mean to save completely, to cure, or to rescue. In other words, it means that Jesus went beyond just saving our souls, He wants to bring salvation to every part of us—even our bodies!

Think about it—if Jesus can do the greatest miracles of forgiving us for *all* of our sins, then healing is a small thing! Just like Jesus brought completeness and forgiveness to our spirits so that we could have a relationship with God again, He wants to make our bodies complete and well too (Matt. 8:17).

Expect Jesus to make you well when you're sick. Expect Him to make you well when your feelings have been wounded. He can even heal friendships that aren't doing very well. And do you know why? Because the Lord has promised to be our healer (Ex. 15:26).

No Other Name

RG
Robert Gay
No oth-er name but the name of Je-sus, no oth-er
name but the name of the Lord; No oth-er name but the name of
last time to Coda
Je - sus is wor - thy of glo - ry, and wor - thy of hon - or, and
wor - thy of pow - er and all praise. No oth - er praise. His
name is ex - alt - ed far a - bove the earth, His
name is high a - bove the heav - ens; His name is ex - alt - ed
far a - bove the earth, give glo - ry and hon - or and
D.S. al Coda
praise un - to His name. No oth - er
Coda
Fine
wor - thy of pow - er and all praise.

My favorite subject when I was in school was history. How about you? What is your favorite subject and why do you like it? (No fair saying recess!) I'll tell you why I like history: it tells us where we've come from, it helps us see what has caused things to be the way they are today, and it helps define the things that we stand for. For example, when we know about the lives of George Washington, Paul Revere, and Benjamin Franklin, and what they sacrificed to see our nation be born, we understand better what our country stands for: freedom to govern ourselves, freedom to worship God, and freedom to talk about what we think.

Because I like history, I also like finding out about the history of the church for many of the same reasons. But there is one additional reason that I like learning about church history: it helps us see the faithfulness of God. He is always faithful to those who trust and love Him. He is always faithful to bring people to Himself. He is always faithful to show Himself fresh and new to every generation and to everyone who will be open to Him. To do that, He sends what people call "revivals." The word "revive" means to renew or awaken, and each time the Lord sends a revival, He renews believers' love for Himself and awakens unbelievers to see their need of Him.

In the 1960s and 1970s, there was a revival in the church called the Jesus Movement. During this time, thousands and thousands of people came to know the Lord. A lot of the people who were coming to know Jesus were young people who had been involved in drugs, lawlessness, and rebellion against any authority. But during the Jesus Movement, the Lord not only brought those people to salvation, but He began making them free from those things that were ruining their lives. At the same time the Lord was bringing many unbelievers to Himself, He was working in the lives of people who were already believers by renewing the importance of worship in the people of God.

One day, a young pastor named Roy Hicks was at his church praying. God had been doing a remarkable thing in the church he pastored, and it had grown to be thousands of people! Many young people were coming to the Lord. As Roy was praying, he was amazed all over again with the fact that it's Jesus who gives us everything! It's Jesus who gives us new life! It's Jesus who gives us freedom! It's Jesus who gives us purpose for our lives!

Roy wanted to write a song that would help his congregation praise the Lord for all of those things! So he wrote the song, "Praise the Name of Jesus." He based his song on Psalm 18:2 which says that the Lord is our rock (our place of security), our fortress (our place of safety), and our deliverer (our place of freedom). Today, let's do what Roy's song says: let's praise the name of Jesus because He has done all those things for us!

Praise the Name of Jesus

Roy Hicks, Jr.

Praise the name of Je - sus, Praise the name of Je - sus.

He's my Rock, He's my Fort-ress, He's my De - liv - er - er, in

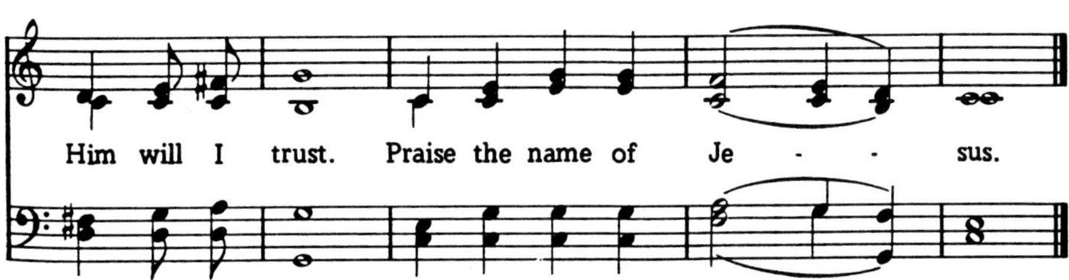
Him will I trust. Praise the name of Je - - sus.

May: The Church's Birth

Charles Wesley was a man who loved God. He had grown up in a home that honored the Lord, he had told people about the Lord in the schools he attended, and he had even gone to the United States (when it was still just a group of colonies) as a missionary. Soon after he returned to England, however, he had an experience with the Lord that he called a "conversion." People can get all worked up about words . . . what one person means by a word can mean something else to someone else. Plus, words are used differently in different centuries. The dictionary gives this definition of the word "conversion": "to change from one form or use to another, or to transform." In Charles' case, he used the word "conversion" because he had an encounter with God that transformed and changed him. Simply put, Charles experienced a life-changing event!

Today people use the word "conversion" to only mean asking Jesus into your heart . . . that certainly is a life-changing event! However, Charles used it to describe an event that happened *after* Jesus already lived in his heart, but that had such an effect on his life it was never the same again!

God wants to do the same kind of thing in us—He wants to keep on changing us even *after* Jesus lives in our hearts. Jesus talked to Nicodemus about being born again (John 3:16). But what do you think would happen if *you* were born and then never grew? Maybe you have a baby brother or sister in your family. What would it be like if they never grew or changed after they were born? Something would be desperately wrong with that baby, and your parents would probably spend a lot of time with the doctor trying to find out what it was.

It's the same thing when we've been born into God's family. Father God is as happy about our "new birth" (asking Jesus into our hearts) as our parents were when we were born. But now He expects us to grow in our spirits just like we grow in our bodies. That's what happened to Charles.

Charles' life was so changed after this experience with the Lord that he and his brother, John, started preaching with new enthusiasm. Their passion for the Lord began a great revival that inspired an entire nation and later came to be called "The Great Awakening" because so many people "woke up" to the fact that they needed to be saved from sin and serve the Lord.

A lot of Charles' sharing about the Lord was through his music. This song, "O for a Thousand Tongues to Sing," reminds us that what Jesus is doing in us is so great that if each of us had a thousand mouths to sing His praise continually, it wouldn't be enough to thank Him or to tell others of everything He's done for us!

O for a Thousand Tongues to Sing

Charles Wesley

Arr. by Lowell Mason

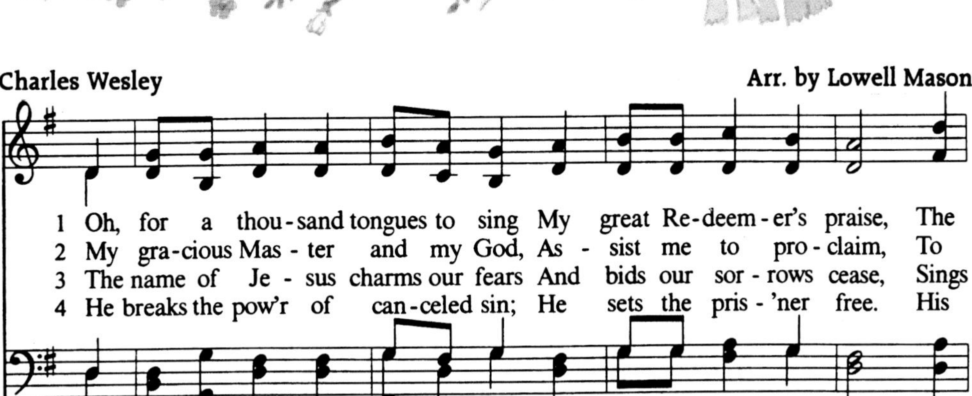
1 Oh, for a thou-sand tongues to sing My great Re-deem-er's praise, The
2 My gra-cious Mas-ter and my God, As-sist me to pro-claim, To
3 The name of Je-sus charms our fears And bids our sor-rows cease, Sings
4 He breaks the pow'r of can-celed sin; He sets the pris-'ner free. His

glo-ries of my God and King, The tri-umphs of his grace!
spread through all the earth a-broad The hon-ors of your name.
mu-sic in the sin-ner's ears, Brings life and health and peace.
blood can make the foul-est clean; His blood a-vails for me.

Jack Hayford had been to an exciting conference where the theme song had been "To God Be the Glory." When he got back home, he found himself singing that song over and over and over—he couldn't get it out of his mind! He was filled with praise for what the Lord had done in his heart at the meetings he had attended. But as beautiful as that theme song was, and as joyously as he sang it, Jack felt like something was missing. He wanted to find a *personal* expression of praise to God—something that flowed out of his own heart, in his own words.

One day as he was coming home from his office, he was overwhelmed by the beauty of the wind-blown sky and autumn trees before him. Praise began to fill his heart again for the beauty of God's creation, and the song "We Lift Our Voice Rejoicing" began to pour forth. The song took a very short time to complete as Jack continued to praise the Lord that afternoon, and the song that we now share together was Jack's personal expression of praise to God for that moment.

God wants to do that same thing in all of us: He wants to give each one of us new and personal expressions of praise for each day. God is very creative! He never wants us to rely only on things He's done in the past, so He's always doing new things!

The Bible says that the Lord wants to begin new things in our lives right now (Isa. 43:19), that His care for us is new every day (Lam. 3:22-23), and that He has provided "a new and living way" for us to come to Him through Jesus (Heb. 10:20). He tells us that once we ask Jesus into our hearts He makes us new people (2 Cor. 5:17), He gives us a new heart, a new spirit (Ezek. 36:26), and a new name! (Rev. 3:12) He even promises that He will eventually make *all* things new (Rev. 21:5).

That newness doesn't just come from God's side, though. While He's doing new things in us, the Bible says that we are supposed to give the Lord new praise every day! We are called to "sing to the Lord a new song, and His praise from the ends of the earth" (Isa. 42:10). The psalmist tells the Lord, "I will sing aloud of Your mercy in the morning" (Ps. 59:16). He later adds, I will "declare Your loving-kindness in the morning, and Your faithfulness every night" (92:2).

What are the new things God is doing in your life right now? Lift *your* voice with rejoicing and thank Him! Having trouble thinking of something? Look around you. What do you see of the beauty of God's work in nature? In your friends? In your family? Have you learned something new from the Bible or in Sunday School? How about school? Is the Lord helping you there? Thank Him for His help! And that tough situation? How is the Lord solving it? Bring all of those things to the Lord and let Him give you new praise for today—just like Jack did. Maybe you will *sing* your praise to the Lord; maybe you will *speak* your praise to Him. But either way, thank the Lord for new things every day!

We Lift Our Voice Rejoicing

J. W. H.
Jack W. Hayford
1. We lift our voice re - joic - ing, Be - cause the Lord a - bove
2. We lift our eyes in faith to The cross where-on He died,
3. We lift our hearts to wor - ship The con-quering Sav-iour's name.
Hath sent His Son to save us, And man - i - fest His love.
Re - deemed at match-less price, now In Christ we're just - i - fied.
Our tongues speak forth the prais - es Of Him who is the same.
Let ev - ery hill re - ech - o With this the song we raise,
His blood hath washed our gar - ments, His peace hath filled our souls,
Christ Je - sus reigns in pow - er Through-out e - ter - ni - ty.
"To Him whose blood hath bought us Be glo - ry, pow'r and praise."
The cross is now our glo - ry Since grace hath made us whole.
As yes - ter - day, so now, and For - ev - er He shall be.
Refrain
We praise Thee, O Fa - ther, Un - speak - a - ble our joy,
In Christ our hearts find glo - ry sin's pow'r can - not de - stroy.

Have you ever thought about the different ways we use clapping? At an important celebration, we may stand and clap to show honor and respect for someone. At a ball game, we may clap to show that someone did a good job. We clap in rhythm to music. Children clap simply because they're happy. Sometimes people will give one loud clap to emphasize a point they're making or to get someone's attention.

The Bible talks about how to use clapping too but applies it to our lives with the Lord. First of all, Psalm 47:1 commands us to worship the Lord with our clapping. It says, "Clap your hands, all you peoples! Shout to God with the voice of triumph!" That's kind of like showing honor and respect for the Lord or telling Him that He's done a good job!

In Bible days, clapping was also used to show that two people were making a contract. They would clap their hands together (kind of like a high-five!). This was a signal that they were agreeing (Job 17:3; Prov. 17:18; 22:26). So when we clap our hands to the Lord, we can show that we're agreeing with the promises of God! The Bible also talks about clapping as being a tool of battle and of scorn against an enemy (Job 27:23; Lam. 2:15).

Rodney Johnson is the organist at a church in Los Angeles, California where all of these reasons for clapping were studied. Over the years, Rodney began to understand why clapping was important because he saw what a difference it made in the worship and prayer of the congregation.

One day, Rodney decided that he wanted to write a song that would help people understand why clapping to the Lord is important, and how it is supposed to be used in our lives. As he wrote the song, "We Applaud Your Greatness," the Lord began to remind him of things in his own life. Rodney was reminded that, as a musician, he came to Los Angeles in the first place hoping to hear the applause of people for how great he was. And he had heard some of that! But he found out that it doesn't last very long.

Instead, one of the most important things Rodney learned was to clap for things that last forever! Our applause in worship to our King Jesus lasts because He lives forever! Our applause reminds us that we agree with what the Lord has said in the Bible; and God's Word lasts forever too!

Do you need to clap today? Maybe you need to clap to remind yourself that you really do agree with the promises God gave us in the Bible. Maybe you just feel filled with the joy of the Lord! Maybe you need to clap in praise to the Lord because He does a good job all of the time! But whenever you clap, remember that we need to be clapping for things that last forever.

We Applaud Your Greatness

RJ
Rodney Johnson
I will not give that which costs me noth - ing,
I clap my hands, to show I'm in a-gree - ment
so when I clap my hands in hon-or of the Lord;
with what the Word of God says con-cern-ing me;
I lift my voice in praise and ad - o-ra - tion,
You're King of kings and Lord of lords for-ev - er,
to-geth-er they be-come an in-stru-ment of war. We ap-
with our applause we come to wel-come roy - al - ty.
plaud Your great - ness, we ap - plaud Your might, and we
shout to God in tri - umph as we
set our-selves to fight; Ev - 'ry de - mon trem-bles when they
hear our voic - es raised, joined with loud ap-plause, af-firm-ing You are
wor - thy to be praised

When Jesus sent His disciples out to preach His Good News, He gave them some last-minute instructions. People who study the Bible call this The Great Commission. (A commission means to give power or authority to someone to do a specific job.) In The Great Commission, Jesus told His disciples things to expect to happen as they told others about Him. He also told them about miracles that He would work through their lives. Each of the four Gospel writers gives an account of The Great Commission and each of them is slightly different. This doesn't mean that they were each told separate things, but that different things stood out to each person. When we put them all together, we get a complete picture of what Jesus wants all of us to do in telling others about Him.

Matthew tells us that the disciples were to go to all nations, baptize people in the name of the Father, Son, and Holy Spirit, and teach people to observe God's commands (28:18-20).

Mark directs us again to go into *all* the world, baptizing people. But Jesus also tells His disciples that as they preach, miracles will happen that will help unbelievers see that the power of God is real and true (16:15-18).

Luke teaches the disciples from the Scriptures that salvation had to come through the death of God's Son. Now, again, the disciples are told to go throughout the whole world spreading God's Good News, and Jesus gives the disciples the promise that God's power will be with them to accomplish this task (24:45-48).

John directs the disciples to go in God's peace as they preach the way of salvation. Jesus also reminds them of their need to receive the Holy Spirit before they set out (20:21-23).

When you combine everything the Gospel writers said about The Great Commission, we can learn several important lessons. First, God's message is for everyone. Jesus didn't tell the disciples to just go to two or three places with His message; He said to go everywhere. The Bible uses phrases like "all the world," "to every person," and "all nations." That sounds like everyone to me! Don't be afraid to tell people that Jesus loves them!

We can also learn to expect God's power to help us when we tell people about Jesus. The Bible says that it is the Holy Spirit who helps people see their need of Jesus and to accept God's gift to them (John 16:7-9). If that's true, it's never *our* power that convinces anyone to ask Jesus into their hearts—it's the power of the Holy Spirit helping us.

Then we also need to go in peace. The Lord isn't asking us to go and argue with people until they accept Jesus! Remember, it's the Holy Spirit that works in their hearts. We need to go in the peace of the Lord and let people see by our lives that Jesus can make a difference!

These Signs Shall Follow Them

L.F.W.W.
L.F.W. Woodford.
1. When first the ri - sen Lord of pow'r His cho-sen ones sent
2. No de - mons shall be - fore them stand, No poi - son do them
3. "They shall with oth - er tongues de - clare The won-ders of their
4. Crowned with the flame of Pen - te - cost, A faith-ful, fear - less
5. No word of Thine is void of power; No prom-ise, Lord, is
forth, A charge He gave, that so - lemn hour, To
harm; Nor sub - tle ser - pent in their hand Cause
God; The sick be - neath their hands, by prayer, Shall
band Pro - claimed His Name: a ran - somed host A -
vain. Be this a Pen - te - cos - tal - hour Con -
preach His sav - ing worth. "Go ye," said He, "to
pain or dread a - larm." For Sa - tan's king-dom
rise to prove My Word." So let it be! firm
rose from ev - ry land. The Lord worked with them
firm Thy Word a - gain! Nor can'st Thou fail, Thou
all man - kind, De - clare My Word, and ye shall find.
He o'er - came, To give His peo - ple right to claim:
as His Throne Stands this clear pro - mise to His own:
from on High, His prov - en Word could none de - ny:
art the same As when of old Thou did'st pro - claim:
"These signs shall sure - ly fol - low them Who on My Name be - lieve."
"These signs shall sure - ly fol - low them Who on My Name be - lieve."
"These signs shall sure - ly fol - low them who on My Name be - lieve."
"These signs shall sure - ly fol - low them who on My Name be - lieve."
"These signs shall sure - ly fol - low them Who on My Name be - lieve."

June: Sharing the Good News

I've always thought it's kind of sad that there are people who say they're going to share the Good News of Jesus and who start by telling people, "All have sinned . . . and the wages of sin is death" (Rom. 3:23; 6:23). Of course, those verses do tell us *why* we need salvation, but they sure don't *sound* like good news to people who don't know the whole story of Jesus' coming to save us.

Instead, why don't we tell people the good news of what God wants to do in our lives if we accept His gift? Look at what He's done!

We have forgiveness for all of our sin—big ones and little ones! "Jesus said, 'Father, forgive them, for they don't know what they are doing' "(Luke 23:34). "If we admit our sins to the Lord—the One who is unfailing and fair—He will forgive us and make us clean from all sin" (1 John 1:9).

We have freedom from sin's power over us! "Stand solid in the freedom you have in Jesus, and do not be caught again in the slavery of sin" (Gal. 5:1).

We have abundant life! "I have come to give you life—not just regular life, but life that's better than you thought it could ever be" (John 10:10).

We are a part of God's family! "You are all children of God through faith in Jesus Christ" (Gal. 3:26). "You received the Spirit of adoption so that we can call God Abba [this means Daddy], Father" (Rom. 8:15).

We rule with Jesus! "[God] raised [Jesus] from the dead and seated Him at His right hand in heavenly places, far above . . . everything, now and in the future. And He put all things under Jesus' feet." God also "raised *us* up, and made us sit together in the heavenly places with Christ Jesus" (Eph. 1:20-22; 2:6).

We have godly fruit growing in our lives! "The fruit of the Spirit is love, joy, peace, patience, kindness, goodness, faithfulness, gentleness, self-control" (Gal. 5:22-23).

We are a part of God's kingdom! "He has made us free from darkness and brought us into the kingdom of His Son" (Col. 1:13).

We have power to overcome sin! "The sting of death is sin. . . . But thanks be to God, who gives us the victory through our Lord Jesus Christ" (1 Cor. 15:56-57).

We have eternal life! "God loved the world so much, that He gave us His only Son, so that whoever believes in Him will have eternal life" (John 3:16).

I Love to Tell the Story

A. Catherine Hankey
William G. Fischer
1. I love to tell the sto - ry, Of un - seen things a - bove, Of Je - sus and His glo - ry, Of Je - sus and His love. I love to tell the sto - ry, Be - cause I know 'tis true; It sat - is - fies my long - ings As noth - ing else can do.
2. I love to tell the sto - ry, More won - der - ful it seems Than all the gold - en fan - cies Of all our gold - en dreams. I love to tell the sto - ry, It did so much for me; And that is just the rea - son I tell it now to thee.
3. I love to tell the sto - ry, 'Tis pleas - ant to re - peat What seems, each time I tell it, More won - der - ful - ly sweet. I love to tell the sto - ry, For some have nev - er heard The mes - sage of sal - va - tion From God's own Ho - ly Word.
4. I love to tell the sto - ry, For those who know it best Seem hun - ger - ing and thirst - ing To hear it like the rest. And when, in scenes of glo - ry, I sing the new, new, song, 'Twill be the old, old sto - ry, That I have loved so long.
Refrain
I love to tell the sto - ry, 'Twill be my theme in glo - ry,
To tell the old, old sto - ry Of Je - sus and His love.

The story of the life of John Newton sounds a lot like the story of Robinson Crusoe! It seems like the most incredible, exciting adventure, but in reality it is the story of a man who became a horrible and prideful sinner, and how God finally reached him with His love.

John's life began in England. He had a mother who was very devoted to God, but who died when John was only seven years old, and a father who was a sea captain. After his mother's death, John attended several years of school. But when he turned eleven, John's father took him to sea with him. Several years passed, then one night when they were docked, John was kidnapped and taken aboard a war ship as a sailor in the English Navy.

He was still a young boy and the influence of the older sailors was anything but proper. So John eventually set aside all that his mother had taught him about the Lord and became a very corrupt and wicked person.

As time went by, John became tired of being in the Navy—there were too many rules for him. He wanted to be able to do whatever he wanted and not obey anyone. So he deserted and began working for a man who was a slave trader. They would go up and down the West African coast capturing people. Once the ship was full, they would cross the ocean and sell these people . . . and John learned the business well. He eventually became captain of his own slave ship. Now, John didn't care about God, and he didn't care about people. He only cared about himself and getting whatever he wanted.

One day, there was a terrible storm at sea. Although he was an experienced sailor, John was afraid. The storm went on for days, and John was certain that he would die. In the midst of the storm, he prayed for the first time in years, asking God to have mercy on him. The Lord did have mercy on John and spared his life. Shortly after this, John asked Jesus into his heart.

It took some time for John to get out of the horrible business he was in, but he eventually became a minister, giving his testimony and leading many people to Christ. He also fought hard in England to have the slave trade destroyed. He wrote some beautiful hymns too. The most famous of these is "Amazing Grace."

John Newton, better than anyone else, was able to compose this song because he had an understanding of grace that most of us don't. Grace is forgiveness and mercy that we don't deserve. John knew that he didn't deserve anything from God, and yet God saved him. A short time before he died, John again reminded people about what God had done for him. He said, "Though my memory is failing, I can never forget two things; first, that I was a great sinner, and second, that Jesus is a great Savior." And there is no one beyond God's reach!

Amazing Grace

John Newton

Walker's Southern Harmony

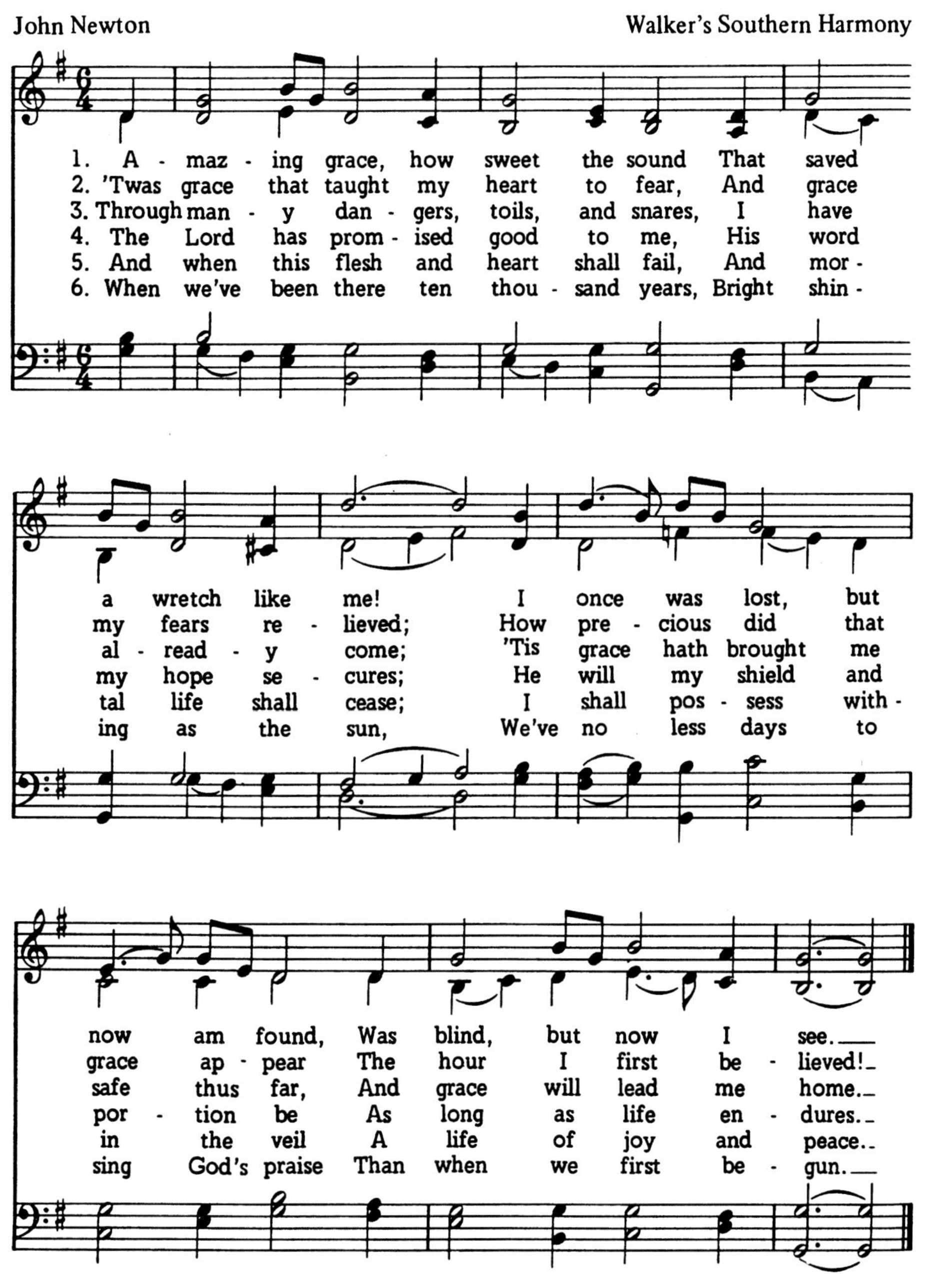
1. A - maz - ing grace, how sweet the sound That saved a wretch like me! I once was lost, but now am found, Was blind, but now I see.
2. 'Twas grace that taught my heart to fear, And grace my fears re - lieved; How pre - cious did that grace ap - pear The hour I first be - lieved!
3. Through man - y dan - gers, toils, and snares, I have al - read - y come; 'Tis grace hath brought me safe thus far, And grace will lead me home.
4. The Lord has prom - ised good to me, His word my hope se - cures; He will my shield and por - tion be As long as life en - dures.
5. And when this flesh and heart shall fail, And mor - tal life shall cease; I shall pos - sess with - in the veil A life of joy and peace.
6. When we've been there ten thou - sand years, Bright shin - ing as the sun, We've no less days to sing God's praise Than when we first be - gun.

Everyone needs to hear the Good News about Jesus! But the reason everyone needs Good News is because something bad took place before that. The bad thing that happened is that sin and rebellion against God came into the hearts of every person through Adam and Eve. When that happened, every person earned death and separation from God forever, because the wages of sin is death (Rom. 6:23). It wasn't possible for us to die for our own sins. Since it would have been a fair punishment to die for our own disobedience, we needed Someone who was sinless and obedient to God—Someone who hadn't earned death—to come and take our place. Only Someone perfect could have taken our punishment and then conquered the devil by rising from the dead. And we couldn't do that for ourselves. So, part of sharing the Good News with people is helping them to recognize their need of Someone to receive sin's punishment in their place.

The Good News is that God knew that we could never do that for ourselves, so He did it for us through Jesus, the Lamb of God! The Bible calls Jesus the Lamb of God because He was our sacrifice—He took our punishment for us and died in our place.

Have you ever wondered why the Bible calls Jesus the Lamb of God? It's because all through the Bible, God used the sacrifice of animals to give us a picture of what He would eventually do through His Son. The very first sacrifice that we read about in the Bible happened in Genesis 3:21. After Adam and Eve sinned, the Bible says that they were naked—they had come out from under God's protection and were uncovered. Their physical nakedness was just a symptom of what had happened to their spirits. So the Bible tells us that God killed an animal and took the skins to cover Adam and Eve. It was a picture for us of what sacrifice was supposed to accomplish: *sacrifice covers and protects us.*

Later, in Exodus, we read about the Passover Lamb. You probably know that story. Moses told the Children of Israel to put the blood of the lamb on their doors. If they obeyed, the angel of death would pass over them and everyone inside would live. This was another picture for us: *sacrifice brings us life.*

In Leviticus 4–6, we learn about "sin offerings." Every year, each Israelite was supposed to bring a lamb as a sacrifice to cover his sins. These sacrifices weren't perfect, though, because they had to be repeated year after year (Heb. 10:1-3). Instead, they gave us another picture: *sacrifice brings us forgiveness.*

All of these pictures pointed ahead to God's perfect sacrifice: Jesus. Because He was perfect, He became the sacrifice (or "lamb") who died for everyone! In fact, when John the Baptist saw Jesus, he said, "Look! It's the Lamb of God who takes away the sin of the whole world!" (John 1:29)

Now, because Jesus was the one perfect sacrifice, everyone in heaven and all of those on earth who believe in Jesus give praise to Him (Rev. 5:9-14). It also says that eventually *every* creature will do the same. But let's start *now* and do what those verses say: let's thank Jesus for being our lamb—the Lamb of God!

All Heaven Declares

N & TR

Noel & Tricia Richards

1. All heav'n de- clares the glo- ry of the ri- sen Lord.
2. I will pro- claim the glo- ry of the ri- sen Lord.

Who can com- pare with the beau- ty of the Lord?
Who once was slain to re- con- cile - man to God.

For- ev- er He will be the Lamb up- on the throne.
For- ev- er You will be the Lamb up- on the throne.

I glad- ly bow my knee and wor- ship Him a- lone.
I glad- ly bow my knee and wor- ship You a- lone.

When I was a little girl, my parents taught me to pray before I went to bed. Of course they taught me to pray for my grandparents, and my brothers and sister. I learned to pray for safety. I prayed for our President, our nation, and the pastor of our church. I prayed for friends. And I prayed that the Lord would help me become the kind of person He wanted me to be so I would be ready when Jesus comes back.

But there was one other thing my parents taught me to pray for. They taught me to pray for the missionaries—that God would bless them, care for them, and help them tell a lot of people about Jesus. I even had a missionary pen pal for quite a while. Why do you think they thought this was so important?

We read that the last thing Jesus said to His disciples before He went back to heaven was, "After you receive power from the Holy Spirit, you will tell people about Me in Jerusalem [the town where they lived], in Judea and Samaria [the places just beyond their town], and in the farthest places of the whole world" (Acts 1:8). That means that every time *any* of us tells someone about Jesus, we're doing what Jesus commanded. But the missionaries have made a sacrifice that most of us haven't: they've gone to live in a place that is unfamiliar, to speak a language that is unfamiliar, and to work with people they don't know. So they need extra prayer: not only to teach many people about Jesus, but also that they won't be lonely for their families, friends, and the things that they are used to. (I had one friend who was a missionary who wrote me a letter and said, "Please send us a jar of peanut butter! We can't find *any* here!" So some of the things missionaries miss are simply things that are familiar.)

The song, "Jesus Saves," was written for a missionary meeting in a Sunday School. It was written to remind people what the missionaries are doing by obeying Jesus' command to "go to the farthest places of the earth." They're going because Jesus is the only way to know God. Jesus said, "I am the way . . . no one comes to the Father except by going through Me" (John 14:6). That's a good reason for us to tell people about Jesus and a good reason for us to pray that the missionaries will do the same thing where they are!

The Bible says, "How beautiful on the mountains [that means they've gone far away] are the feet of those who bring good news [that's the Gospel], who teach peace [remember that Jesus is the Prince of Peace], that tell about salvation, and who say that God rules" (Isa. 52:7). Why don't you stop right now and pray that God will help the missionaries do all of those things wherever they are!

Jesus Saves

Priscilla J. Owens
William J. Kirkpatrick
1. We have heard the joy - ful sound; Je - sus saves! Je - sus saves!
2. Waft it on the roll - ing tide; Je - sus saves! Je - sus saves!
3. Sing a - bove the bat - tle strife, Je - sus saves! Je - sus saves!
4. Give the winds a might - y voice, Je - sus saves! Je - sus saves!
Spread the ti - dings all a - round: Je - sus saves! Je - sus saves!
Tell to sin - ners far and wide: Je - sus saves! Je - sus saves!
By His death and end - less life, Je - sus saves! Je - sus saves!
Let the na - tions now re - joice – Je - sus saves! Je - sus saves!
Bear the news to ev - ery land, Climb the steeps and cross the waves;
Sing, ye is - lands of the sea; Ech - o back, ye o - cean caves;
Sing it soft - ly through the gloom, When the heart for mer - cy craves;
Shout sal - va - tion full and free; High - est hills and deep - est caves;
On - ward! – 'tis our Lord's com - mand; Je - sus saves! Je - sus saves!
Earth shall keep her ju - bi - lee; Je - sus saves! Je - sus saves!
Sing in tri - umph o'er the tomb – Je - sus saves! Je - sus saves!
This our song of vic - to - ry – Je - sus saves! Je - sus saves!

Several years ago, my husband, Scott, had a dream about Jesus coming back to earth. In the dream, it was Christmastime, and Scott saw Jesus far away in the sky, but coming nearer with every second. Jesus looked so beautiful (like a sparkling Christmas tree ornament) and Scott was so excited that he ran out into the street and started shouting to all of our neighbors, "Hear people, everywhere! Jesus Christ has come!" His joy at Jesus' return made it impossible for him to keep quiet! He wanted to share his joy with everyone around, so that they too would be ready to receive Jesus at His second coming.

What a contrast to how I viewed the return of Jesus as a child! I knew that after Jesus rose from the dead, He had gone up in the clouds to heaven, and I knew that an angel told the disciples that "just like you saw Jesus go, He will someday return" (Acts 1:10-11). So I understood that this was a promise to the church and that Jesus *would* someday return. But sometimes I would be in church and the preacher would start talking about Jesus "coming back in the clouds" with "angels and trumpets, and on a white horse." I didn't want it to happen! I was just a kid, but I wanted to grow up and get married and have kids of my own. Besides, the thought of someone coming out of the sky and seeing angels was scary.

But Scott's dream is a lot more like how the Bible describes Jesus' return than what I thought as a child. In fact, the Bible calls the promise of Jesus' return "our blessed hope" (Titus 2:13) because it gives us hope for our future. Without Jesus, none of us have hope for even having a happy life now. That's why everyone who doesn't know Jesus is without hope and without God (Eph. 2:12).

So what is this blessed hope that the Bible talks about? First, we have the hope of again seeing our loved ones who have already died. We will be "caught up together *with them* to meet the Lord" (1 Thes. 4:17). We also have the hope of a place for eternity. Jesus said that He was going to "prepare a place for us" (John 14:2), and I've got to say—I'm looking forward to seeing what it's like! We also have the hope of a reward. When Jesus comes back, He will "reward each person according to what he has done" (Matt. 16:27). That's an exciting thing if what we've been doing is serving and obeying Jesus!

That's a lot to look forward to! But in the meantime, Jesus said for us to be busy with what He's told us to do before He comes back (Luke 19:13). One of those things is telling people about the Lord. If the hope we have in Jesus' coming is so great, no wonder Scott in his dream was shouting and telling everyone to be ready to meet Him! Begin to pray for people your family knows who don't know the Lord and then watch the Lord bring them to Himself so that they too can share in "that blessed hope."

Hear People Everywhere

RLB
Rebecca L. Bauer
1. Hear peo- ple ev- 'ry- where Je- sus Christ has come.
2. Hear peo- ple ev- 'ry- where Je- sus Christ is here.
3. Hear peo- ple ev- 'ry- where Je- sus Christ will come.
Sanc- ti- fy! Pur- i- fy! Your- selves in the blood of the Lamb. Pre-
Lift your praise hands up- raised Your eyes now be- hold- ing His throne! Re-
Fa- ther God calls to- day to find full ac- cept- ance in Him.
pare! Pre- pare! Your hearts to kneel at the throne of His grace.
joice! Re- joice! And join the song of His tri- umph and praise.
Come! O Come! A- bund- ant love is the free gift of God.
Hear peo- ple ev- 'ry- where Je- sus - Christ has come.
Hear peo- ple ev- 'ry- where Je- sus - Christ is here.
Hear peo- ple ev- 'ry- where Je- sus - Christ will come.

July: Rest

One day, Jesus was invited to the home of Mary and Martha. They were so excited! Wouldn't you be excited to have Jesus come to your house? When Jesus got there, Mary was so delighted! She sat with Jesus and talked with Him. She probably asked Him questions and learned many things about what it means to be one of His followers. She was content and happy just to be in Jesus' presence.

But Martha—well, Martha was too busy to be in Jesus' presence. After all, she had a dinner to get on the table! She hustled and bustled around the house, cooking, cleaning up, setting the table, making sure everything was just right.

Finally, Martha had reached her limit. Frustrated, she came to Jesus and said, "Don't You care that I'm doing all the work? Tell Mary to come and help me!" Jesus gently said, "Martha, you are worried about a lot of things, but only one thing is necessary. Mary has chosen that one thing—and it won't be taken away from her" (Luke 10:40-42).

What had Mary learned that Martha hadn't? She had learned to be happy just being with Jesus. She learned what the song, "No Other Plea," tells us. It says, "My faith has found a resting place." Later the song tells us, "It is enough for me that Jesus died and that He died for me."

Nothing is as important as Jesus in our lives. But sometimes we forget that because so many things are going on around us. Our lives are filled with school, chores, homework, video games, TV, friends, baseball, dance classes, soccer, basketball, Sunday School, choir, extra school activities, gymnastics, music lessons—whew! With all of that going on, it's easy to forget that we're supposed to be in that "resting place" of Jesus' presence. It's also easy to forget to spend time learning more about what Jesus has done for us. Spending time with Jesus doesn't mean that we don't go to school or that we'll never do another chore or play another game. But it does mean that we need to set aside time for Him every day.

How do you think we should do that? Are there ways that you spend time every day with Jesus now? There are two very important ones that everyone should do: we should read our Bibles every day and we should pray every day. The Apostle Peter says that reading the Bible is our spiritual food, so if we aren't reading our Bibles, it's like starving our spirits (Ps. 119:103; 1 Peter 2:2). And prayer gives us a time not only to talk to the Lord but also to let Him talk to us (Ps. 5:3; Dan. 6:10).

The Bible says, "Be still and know that I am God" (Ps. 46:10). It's a reminder to not let all the other things in our lives crowd Jesus out. It's also a reminder that being in Jesus' presence is supposed to be a very important part of our lives.

No Other Plea

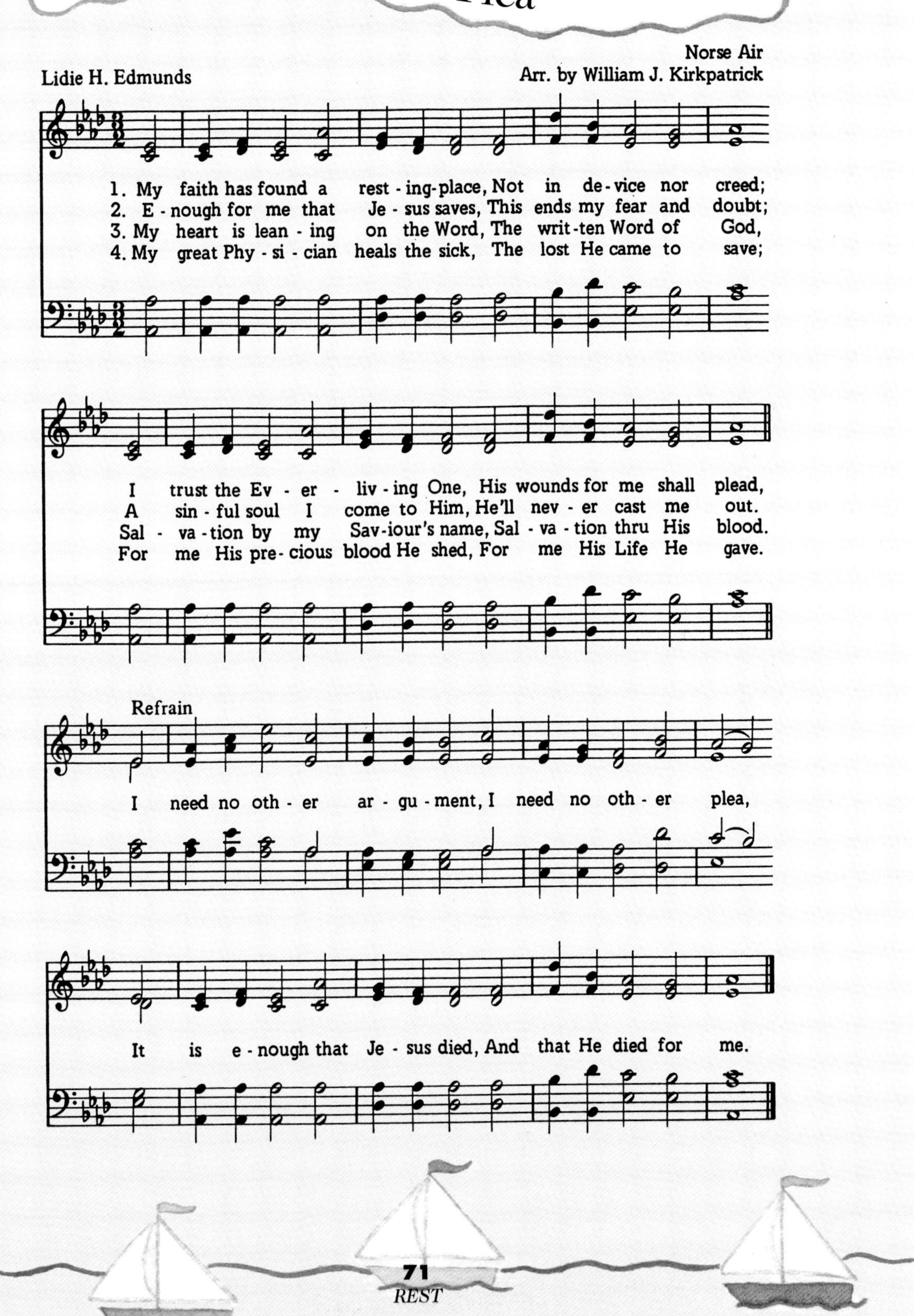
Norse Air
Lidie H. Edmunds
Arr. by William J. Kirkpatrick
1. My faith has found a rest - ing-place, Not in de - vice nor creed;
2. E - nough for me that Je - sus saves, This ends my fear and doubt;
3. My heart is lean - ing on the Word, The writ - ten Word of God,
4. My great Phy - si - cian heals the sick, The lost He came to save;
I trust the Ev - er - liv - ing One, His wounds for me shall plead,
A sin - ful soul I come to Him, He'll nev - er cast me out.
Sal - va - tion by my Sav - iour's name, Sal - va - tion thru His blood.
For me His pre - cious blood He shed, For me His Life He gave.
Refrain
I need no oth - er ar - gu - ment, I need no oth - er plea,
It is e - nough that Je - sus died, And that He died for me.

Mr. and Mrs. Crosby were going to have a baby! What a joyful time! Like any family, they planned for their new baby. They prepared a nursery and made clothes. They got diapers. Then when everything was ready, they settled back to wait for that special day which finally arrived on March 24, 1823, when their beautiful baby daughter was born. They named her Frances Jane, and gave her the nickname of "Fanny." Everything went well for the first six weeks of Fanny's life, but then she caught a cold which caused an eye inflammation. Mr. and Mrs. Crosby called the doctor to come and take a look at Fanny's eyes. The doctor, however, made a terrible mistake and put the wrong medicine in Fanny's eyes. The wrong medicine made Fanny lose her sight and she was blind for the rest of her life.

What for some would have been an unbearable tragedy, however, Fanny conquered! Although she never regained her sight, she went to school and learned and began to show a remarkable gift for writing poetry. She also developed a very close relationship with the Lord and loved Him with all of her heart. She said, "Darkness may throw a shadow over my outer vision, but there is no cloud that can keep the sunlight of hope from a trustful soul." She even went so far as to pronounce her blindness a blessing! She said in her later years that she believed God had used her sightlessness to set her apart for the ministry of writing music for the people of God. She *did* do that too! In her lifetime, she wrote over 8,000 hymns, and she wrote her first one when she was only eight years old!

One of her most famous hymns is "Blessed Assurance," in which Fanny wrote about the certainty of our salvation and the joy it brings to each one of us. One day, a friend of Fanny's came over and played some music she had written. She was hoping Fanny would write some words to go with her music. After she had played the music for Fanny, she turned to her and said, "What does that music say to you?" Fanny smiled and said immediately, "It says, 'Blessed assurance! Jesus is mine'!"

Fanny died just one month before her 95th birthday. But at her 90th birthday celebration, she said, "There is nothing in this wide world that gives me so much joy as telling the story of my Savior's loving mercy:

This is my story, this is my song,
Praising my Savior all the day long. Hallelujah!

My love for the Holy Bible and its sacred truth is stronger and more precious to me at ninety than at nineteen."

Fanny knew that the most important thing in life isn't being famous, or having a lot of money, or even being able to see. The most important thing is knowing that Jesus is in your life.

Blessed Assurance

Fanny J. Crosby
Phoebe P. Knapp
1. Bless-ed as - sur-ance, Je - sus is mine! O, what a fore-taste of glo - ry di - vine! Heir of sal - va - tion, pur - chase of God, Born of His Spir - it, washed in His blood.
2. Per - fect sub - mis-sion, per - fect de - light, Vi-sions of rap - ture now burst on my sight; An-gels de - scend - ing, bring from a - bove Ech - oes of mer - cy, whis-pers of love.
3. Per - fect sub - mis-sion, all is at rest, I in my Sav - ior am hap - py and blest; Watch-ing and wait - ing, look - ing a - bove, Filled with His good - ness, lost in His love.
Refrain
This is my sto - ry, this is my song, Prais-ing my Sav - ior all the day long; This is my sto - ry, this is my song, Prais - ing my Sav - ior all the day long.

Near where my children play baseball there is a big vacant field. Once a year, a carnival comes and fills this field up with rides, booths, food concessions, and bright lights. When I was a little girl, the same kind of thing would come every year where I lived too, except they used the supermarket parking lot.

In a way these carnivals remind me of life without the Lord. People who don't have the Lord in their lives are always trying to find fun and excitement in life. The only way they know to do that is to make everything more wild than when they did it the last time. Like some people at the carnival. They try to go on scarier rides. They try to eat more than they did last time. They run to each attraction trying to fit more in than they did the time before.

The problem with a carnival is that as much fun as it seems to be at the moment, there comes a time when you get tired. You're ready to go home and rest. All of a sudden the crowd and noise that seemed so fun at the beginning gets irritating. You get tired of getting bumped by all of the people around, and the noise makes your head hurt. Maybe your stomach is upset from all of that cotton candy, and . . . it's just time to go home.

That's how people without the Lord live their whole lives. They spend a lot of time trying to find something that will make them happy, but it's never enough. So they run to the next thing. Eventually all of that running only winds up making them tired. And when they get tired, they don't have a "home" to go to.

The Lord solves that problem by offering us true rest in Himself. We are commanded to "rest in the Lord" (Ps. 37:7). And God's rest will give us rest for our souls (Jer. 6:16). Later Jesus said, "Come to Me . . . and I will give you rest" (Matt. 11:28).

But there are some other things to understand about our resting place in the Lord. When we come to the Lord, where He sits (or rests) is on the "throne of His holiness" (Ps. 47:8). Once we have Jesus in our hearts, we find out that God "has made us sit with Christ in heavenly places" (Eph. 2:6). So where we ultimately find true rest is by accepting Jesus and then being seated with Him in heavenly places . . . at the throne of His holiness.

The idea of "holiness" scares a lot of people. They think that if they try to become "holy" they will have to be some kind of a "goody-goody." It seems really fake to them to work it out on their own. But actually, the word holiness is a lot like the word "wholeness" or "completeness." When we come to the Lord, His "wholeness" makes us "complete" so that we don't have to run around looking for something to satisfy us . . . we already have it! We can rest in what Jesus has done and is doing for us. The Bible says that we "are complete in Him [Jesus]" (Col. 2:10), and that God will provide everything that we have need of (Phil. 4:19). He can do that because He is complete—holy. And He wants to make us more complete every day!

Hide Me In Your Holiness

Steve Ragsdale

SR
Steve Ragsdale
Hide me, Lord, in Your ho - li - ness,
ev - 'ry sin I now con - fess.
Praise to_ You. ______for - giv - ing_ Lord,
hide me in Your ho - li - ness, ______
hide me in Your ho - li - ness. ______

The Bible shows God to us in three ways: the Father, the Son, and the Holy Spirit. We call this Three-in-one God the Trinity. Understanding the idea of the Trinity can be rather difficult, but there is one example that can help us understand it a little bit. An egg has three parts: the shell, the white, and the yolk, but together they make only one egg. When you take one part away, we call it a different name, but it's still *all* part of the egg. In the same way, the Father, the Son, and the Holy Spirit are all one. Even though we call them by different names, it doesn't make them any less God or any less a part of the complete God. Let's look at each member of the Trinity and what He does in our lives.

First there is the Father. He provides us with security and His constant presence. For some people that's hard to imagine because, in our world today, many fathers leave their children. For some children, their father has died. But that will never happen with God. In fact, the Bible calls Him the Everlasting Father (Isa. 9:6). He will never, ever leave us. Psalms even says that God will be "a father to the fatherless" (68:5). Later, God is revealed by one more name: Abba Father (Rom. 8:15). Abba is the word used in Jesus' time that meant "Daddy." Father God isn't just "a big man" who rules in the heavens and occasionally checks in on us; He's *Daddy* God . . . the One whose lap you can climb onto when you're lonely or afraid; the One whose arms you can fall asleep in and feel completely safe, protected, and loved.

Jesus is revealed to us as the Son, and we know that He's the One who came to bring us the gift of salvation. But not only did Jesus come to save us, He calls us His friends (John 15:15). What do you do with your friends? You talk to them, you tell them your secrets. Sooner than anybody else, your friends will know if something has hurt your feelings or made you sad, and they are there to encourage and love you. They're also the first ones to know if anything has made you happy and they're there to share in your joy!

Finally, there is the Holy Spirit. Just like there are nicknames for Jesus in the Bible, there are nicknames for the Holy Spirit. One of them is the Comforter (14:26). The Bible also gives us a picture of the Holy Spirit as a dove, which is the symbol of peace (Mark 1:10). When I think of needing comfort, I think of my mom. Friends may be for sharing, but moms are definitely for comfort: they're the ones who bring out the first-aid cream and Band-Aid. They're the ones who have lunch ready on a cold, stormy day. And as soon as you're with them, you just know everything will be all right! That's my picture of the Holy Spirit! He will always be there to bind up hurts, to feed us from the Word of God (John 14:26), and to bring peace in any situation.

Lean on God. Spend time with Him in prayer. He is always there for you—if you need to sit on His lap, if you need to tell Him a joy or sorrow, or if you just need to be in the peace of His presence.

Come Thou Almighty King

Source unknown

Felice de Giardini

1. Come, Thou Al - might - y King, Help us Thy name to sing,
2. Come, Thou In - car - nate Word, Gird on Thy might - y sword,
3. Come, Ho - ly Com - fort - er, Thy sa - cred wit - ness bear
4. To Thee, great One in Three, E - ter - nal prais - es be

Help us to praise: Fa - ther, all glo - ri - ous, O'er all vic-
Our prayer at - tend: Come, and Thy peo - ple bless, And give Thy
In this glad hour: Thou who al - might - y art, Now rule in
Hence, ev - er - more! Thy sov - ereign maj - es - ty May we in

to - ri - ous, Come, and reign o - ver us, An - cient of Days.
word suc - cess: Spir - it of ho - li - ness, On us de - scend.
ev - 'ry heart, And ne'er from us de - part, Spir - it of pow'r.
glo - ry see, And to e - ter - ni - ty Love and a - dore! A - men.

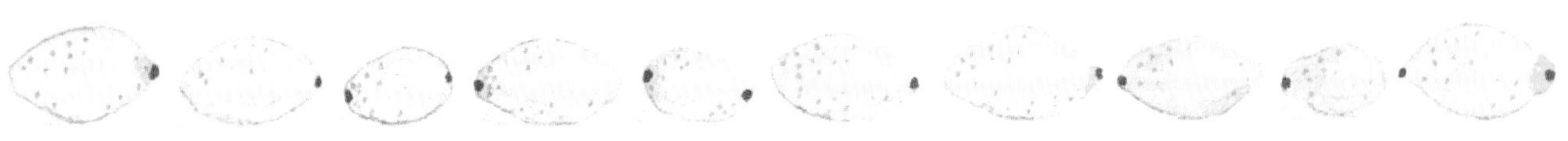

August: Comfort in Trial

Horatio Spafford was a very wealthy and successful man. He had a thriving business, a beautiful home, a wife who loved him, and four lovely daughters. In 1873, he and his wife decided to take the whole family on a trip to Great Britain. In those days, there weren't airplanes for really fast travel. The fastest way to travel was by boat. So Horatio bought tickets for his family on the steamship, *S.S. Ville de Havre.* Just before they were to leave, however, Horatio was suddenly called on to take care of some urgent business and couldn't leave when planned. So he sent his wife and daughters on ahead and arranged to follow them as soon as possible.

The trip was going along nicely, and Mrs. Spafford and the four girls had almost reached their destination when disaster struck. Off the coast of Ireland, their ship collided with another ship and began to go down. The tragedy was swift and the ship sank in only twelve minutes with almost everyone on board perishing.

In those twelve minutes, however, Mrs. Spafford kept her wits about her. As any mother would, she looked after her daughters first. She quickly gathered them on the deck. There they knelt briefly in prayer, entrusting themselves to God. Then she immediately got them into a lifeboat. The boat didn't have room for Mrs. Spafford, so she stayed behind, waiting for the next one. It was the last time that she ever saw her daughters, for unknown to her, their lifeboat began to have difficulty and also sank.

Mrs. Spafford eventually reached land safely and awaited word of her family. When she finally found out that her daughters' boat had sunk, she was grief-stricken. She sent a telegram to Horatio which said, "Saved alone." Horatio, of course, was also overwhelmed with grief, describing it later in his song, "When sorrows like sea billows roll." He joined his wife as soon as he could, but, of course, the fastest way to get to her was by ship. As he neared the place where he was told the *Ville de Havre* had gone down, in his grief and crying out to God, he wrote this beautiful song, "It Is Well With My Soul," because Horatio knew something that gave him great comfort and hope. Shortly before his wife and daughters had set sail, his daughters had all accepted Christ as their Savior at a meeting conducted by D.L. Moody—a famous evangelist. (He would have been to them what Billy Graham is to us.) So Horatio didn't "sorrow like those who have no hope" (1 Thes. 4:13). Horatio knew that the most important issue for anyone is what they do with their soul. His daughters had made their choice and so Horatio had that hope—and the joy of knowing they would spend forever together in heaven.

Have you ever had a loved one die? I have. It's a terrible experience. But in the midst of it, we too can trust in God's promises. The Bible doesn't say we don't sorrow at all . . . it says we don't sorrow like those without hope, because we *do* have hope—and it goes beyond this life!

Sugar

It Is Well With My Soul

Horatio G. Spafford
Philip P. Bliss
1. When peace like a riv - er at - tend - eth my way, When
2. Though Sa - tan should buf - fet, tho' tri - als should come, Let
3. My sin, O, the bliss of this glo - ri - ous thought, My
4. And Lord, haste the day when the faith shall be sight, The
sor - rows like sea - bil - lows roll; What - ev - er my
this blest as - sur - ance con - trol, That Christ has re -
sin not in part but the whole, Is nailed to the
clouds be rolled back as a scroll, The trump shall re -
lot, Thou hast taught me to say, "It is well, it is
gard - ed my help - less es - tate, And hath shed His own
cross and I bear it no more, Praise the Lord, praise the
sound and the Lord shall de - scend, "E - ven so," it is
Refrain
well with my soul."
blood for my soul. It is well with my
Lord, O my soul! It is well
well with my soul.
soul, It is well, it is well with my soul.
with my soul,

HAMBURGERS ♥ CHICKEN ♥ DODGER DOGS ♥ FOIL-WRAPPED TATERS

Have you ever been in a room and had someone accidentally turn the light out on you? It takes a minute for your eyes to get adjusted to the dark so that you can find your way out, but for that minute you can feel very startled and confused, maybe even a little scared. But then, you see the little sliver of light under the door and you know which way to go . . . toward the light! What a relief to be back where everyone else is, where there's warmth, light, and people!

When bad or sad things happen, we can feel that same way on the inside—confused and scared. But the solution is the same . . . go toward the light! Jesus is the light of the world (John 8:12), so when we face a situation that is filled with sadness and seems, well . . . dark, we need to go to Jesus and He will bring that same sense of comfort to us.

That's what Don Moen learned through a tragic event that took place in his family. One night, he received a telephone call letting him know that one of his nephews, Jeremy, had been killed and three other nephews injured in a terrible car accident.

As he was traveling to be with his family, Don began asking the Lord for words of comfort to share in the middle of that very dark situation. The Lord gave Don these words: "God will make a way where there seems to be no way . . . He works in ways we cannot see."

Does this mean that God made the accident happen? No. The Bible teaches that nothing bad ever comes from God's hand (James 1:17). But because we live in a world that is held captive by sin and Satan, bad things *do* happen. In fact, the Bible describes Satan as a roaring lion looking for ways to steal, kill, and destroy anything he can (1 Peter 5:8; John 10:10).

What's wonderful about God is that *in the middle* of something bad, He will bring about something redemptive. That's a big word that means: to rescue, buy back, or set free by paying a ransom. Have you ever heard someone say the phrase, "They really saved the day!" That's what Jesus does in the middle of difficult times.

Have you or your family ever faced an especially "dark" situation? Or are you now? Jesus *is* the answer. Just like God used the testimony of Jeremy's death to bring many people to salvation and the truth of Don's song to comfort many people in the midst of trial, He will bring hope, comfort, and *redemption* in the middle of whatever you face too!

RIBS ♥ BARBECUE ♥ Mm mm! ♥ STEAKS ♥ CORN on the COB ♥ KABOBS

God Will Make A Way

DM
Don Moen
God will make a way where there seems to be no way,
He works in ways we can-not see, He will make a way
for me; He will be my guide, hold me
close-ly to His side, with love and strength for
each new day, He will make a way,
He will make a way.

One way we learn how to live our lives as believers in Jesus is by watching how God works in other people's lives, especially in hard times. It's easy to trust God when everything is going well. But when things are tough—when that bully at school is being mean, or the kid next to you keeps breaking your crayons, or someone makes fun of you, it's harder to see God working in your life. That's true for everybody.

I'll give you an example. When I mentioned the kid breaking crayons, I was talking about something that really happened to my son when he was in the third grade. Brian was excited for the new school year and he arrived that first day with all of his beautiful, perfect, brand-new school supplies. Then, just a of couple weeks into the school year, the boy next to him broke every single crayon Brian had! Of course, Brian wasn't very happy about it and felt angry and picked on. We encouraged Brian to pray for this boy. And we prayed with him too—for the whole year. It didn't seem like anything ever changed.

Well, the next school year started and the boy wasn't there. We found out later that he had moved away. During that frustrating third-grade year the boy's parents had gotten a divorce because the father was addicted to drugs. That boy's life had been in total confusion. I don't know what ever happened to the boy, but the situation taught my son a very valuable lesson: people do broken things because there are broken places in their hearts. It taught Brian to be more compassionate and understanding, and to pray for people, not just get angry.

What happened with Brian can be an example to you about how to pray for other people. In the same way, we can learn from the lives of people we read about in Scripture. The Bible says that the things and people in the Bible are written for a reason: to be examples to teach us how we're supposed to live (1 Cor. 10:11).

The song, "Guide Me, O Thou Great Jehovah," tells about one big example the Bible gives us—the Israelites when they were wandering in the wilderness. They faced hunger, thirst, battles, and uncertainty. They didn't know where they were going to live from one day to the next, but they knew that eventually they would reach the place God had promised them. But even though the journey was tough, God provided everything they needed: food (the manna), water from the rock, protection from their enemies, and direction through the pillar of cloud and of fire.

God will do the same thing for you. Whenever you face something that seems too hard to handle—whether it's something like Brian and the crayons or the Israelites wondering where their next meal would come from—the Lord will meet you there and will take you safely through it. Just do what the song says and ask the Lord to be your "strength and shield." And He will.

Guide Me, O Thou Great Jehovah

William Williams
Welsh Hymn Melody
1. Guide me, O Thou great Je - ho - vah, Pil - grim through this
2. O - pen now the crys - tal foun - tain, Whence the heal - ing
3. When I tread the verge of Jor - dan, Bid my anx - ious
bar - ren land; I am weak, but Thou art might - y; Hold me with Thy
stream doth flow; Let the fire and cloud - y pil - lar Lead me all my
fears sub - side; Bear me thru' the swell - ing cur - rent, Land me safe on
power - ful hand; Bread of Heav - en, Bread of Heav - en, Feed me
jour - ney through; Strong De - liv - 'rer, Strong De - liv - 'rer, Be Thou
Ca - naan's side; Songs of prais - es, songs of prais - es I will
till I want no more, Feed me till I want no more.
still my strength and shield, Be Thou still my strength and shield.
ev - er give to Thee, I will ev - er give to Thee. A - men.

It all began about 500 years ago. In the German town of Wittenberg there lived a young Catholic priest named Martin Luther. Martin began to notice that the church required people to work and sometimes even give money to make sure their sins would be forgiven. One day as he was reading his Bible, he read, "The just shall live by faith" (Rom. 1:17). All of a sudden the truth of that verse dawned in Martin's heart: you didn't have to work hard to be saved; you didn't have to pay money to be saved; Jesus had done it all already and we only had to have faith in Him!

Martin began to challenge these practices and along the way faced challenges of his own from leaders in the church who thought he was a "heretic" (a rebellious person who believes things that aren't in the Bible). Eventually he was removed from the priesthood and started the Protestant Reformation. (Notice "protest" in the word protestant. They were called this because they were protesting against the unbiblical practices of these church leaders.)

Although he faced many difficulties, Martin learned something which he wrote about in the hymn, "A Mighty Fortress Is Our God": we can never face hard things alone, because *our* strength isn't enough. Our strength and protection must come from the Lord.

Martin described Jesus as "Lord Sabaoth." That's a Hebrew word that means "armies ready for war." The idea behind this name of Jesus is that He is Captain of the Lord's army and He is ready to go to battle for us and defend us. If that's true, then God is the surest refuge—the most dependable shelter—that we have. He is "a bulwark (a wall of protection) never failing."

Look at these verses about God being our mighty fortress:

"The Lord is my rock and my fortress and my rescuer; He is my God, my strength, the one I trust in; He is my shield and my strong savior, my stronghold" (Ps. 18:2).

"In You, Lord, I put my trust . . . be my rock of refuge, a fortress of protection to save me" (31:1-2).

"In God is my salvation and my glory; the rock of my strength, and my refuge is in God" (62:7).

"Blessed be the Lord who is my Rock . . . He is my shield and the One in whom I take refuge" (144:1-2).

And here is the verse that Martin based his song on: "God is our refuge and strength, a helper who is there during trouble" (46:1).

Now, the next time you face trouble, you'll know where to go for safety!

A Mighty Fortress Is Our God

Martin Luther
Trans. by Frederick H. Hedge
Martin Luther
1. A mighty - y For - tress is our God, A Bul - wark nev - er
2. Did we in our own strength con-fide, Our striv - ing would be
3. And tho' this world, with dev - ils filled, Should threat - en to un-
4. That word a - bove all earth - ly powers, No thanks to them, a-
fail - ing; Our Help - er He, a - mid the flood Of
los - ing, Were not the right Man on our side, The
do us, We will not fear, for God hath willed His
bid - eth; The Spir - it and the gifts are ours Thru
mor - tal ills pre - vail - ing: For still our an - cient foe Doth
Man of God's own choos - ing: Dost ask who that may be? Christ
truth to tri - umph through us; The Prince of Dark - ness grim, We
Him who with us sid - eth; Let goods and kin - dred go, This
seek to work us woe; His craft and power are great, And
Je - sus, it is He; Lord Sab - a - oth His name, From
trem - ble not for him; His rage we can en - dure, For
mor - tal life al - so; The bod - y they may kill: God's
armed with cru - el hate, On earth is not his e - qual.
age to age the same, And He must win the bat - tle.
lo, his doom is sure; One lit - tle word shall fell him.
truth a - bid - eth still; His King-dom is for - ev - er. A - men.

September: Growth

Have you ever noticed what the water in your dog's bowl looks like at the end of a summer day? You put clean water in the bowl in the morning—it's cool, clean, and refreshing. But by the end of the day, it's lukewarm, dusty, and well, *yucky*! There needs to be new water put in that bowl! There's another word to describe that kind of yucky water: stagnant.

"Stagnant" is used to describe water that isn't flowing and clear but that has become dirty and slow moving. Stagnant can also be used to describe people who have become disinterested, sluggish, or inactive; kind of like couch potatoes! Did you know, though, that we can become couch potatoes in our spirits too? We can become used to God in our lives, or tired of reading our Bibles, or indifferent about going to church. When that happens, we need to be renewed and refreshed by God's Spirit.

This song, "Revive Us Again," is a reminder of why our joy in the Lord and our desire to love, serve, and praise Him should be new and vital every day! "We praise Thee, O Lord, for the Son of Thy love," William Mackay, the composer of this song, wrote. William was a man who felt this way about the Lord—filled with love, praise, and thankfulness. He had studied to be a doctor and was in college when he asked Jesus into his heart. By the time he graduated, however, William was so filled with enthusiasm for the Lord, he knew he would never be happy doing anything other than preaching. He became a pastor, as well as an evangelist, leading many people to the Lord through his preaching and writing.

William wrote this song based on a verse that says, "Lord, revive Your work in the middle of the years" (Hab. 3:2). In other words, the prophet was saying, "Lord, revive Your work in us—NOW! Don't wait any longer!" The Lord always wants to do that for each of us. He wants to revive and renew His work in us every day. The Psalmist even asks the Lord to "Revive us again, so that we may rejoice in You" Hallelujah! (Ps. 85:6).

One way that the Lord renews His work in us is to immerse us in His river of life. God's river of life is a lot like a river of water. You can dip your feet in a little way and then run off and do something else. Or you can go clear out to the middle and swim! In the same way, we can pay attention to God a little—maybe on Sundays at church; or we can make Jesus a part of our everyday life through reading our Bibles, praying, and choosing what God would want us to choose.

Ezekiel wrote about this river of life (Ezek. 47). He talked about wading in up to his ankles, then to his knees, then to his waist, and then deep enough to swim in. Just as God calls us to grow in Him, He also invites us into the center of the river of His life. Accept that invitation today. Just like Ezekiel, let's get into the river! Don't just dabble around the edges . . . it's a lot more fun to swim than to wade!

Revive Us Again

William P. Mackay
John J. Husband
1. We praise Thee, O God! for the Son of Thy love, For Jesus who died, and is now gone above.
2. We praise Thee, O God! for Thy Spirit of light, Who has shown us our Saviour, and scattered our night.
3. All glory and praise to the Lamb that was slain, Who has borne all our sins, and hath cleansed ev'ry stain.
4. Revive us again; fill each heart with Thy love; May each soul be rekindled with fire from above.
Refrain
Hallelujah! Thine the glory, Hallelujah! Amen; Hallelujah! Thine the glory, revive us again.

There was a time in Jesus' life when many people who had followed Him turned away and decided that what He was asking from them was more than they wanted to give to Him. It happened shortly after Jesus had fed the 5,000 people with the five loaves and two fish. Some of the people began to follow Jesus just because He did miracles and provided food for them. Jesus didn't want people to follow Him because He did miracles. He wanted people to follow Him because they loved Him and believed in what He taught. Jesus began to explain to the people that the true bread isn't the kind you eat. He is the true bread—the bread that would fill every person's heart! "For the bread of God is He who comes down from heaven and gives life to the world. . . . I am the bread of life. He who comes to Me shall never hunger, and he who believes in Me shall never thirst" (John 6:33, 35). Many of the people thought that was hard to understand, and John tells us after that many of Jesus' followers left and didn't walk with Him any more (v. 66). Jesus sadly turned to His twelve disciples and asked, "Do you want to go away too?" Peter gave a wonderful answer! He said, "Lord, who shall we go to? Only You have the words of life!" (v. 68)

Peter, in that moment, recognized something that we all need to understand. We can leave Jesus if we want to, and other people will be happy to give us answers for the things we have to do. But only Jesus' answers give us *life*! That's why we need to learn everything we can about Him. That sounds like a pretty big project, doesn't it! But the Bible tells us how to start out!

First, we need to ask the Lord to help us learn. The psalmwriter prays, "Show me Your ways, O Lord, teach me Your paths, lead me in Your truth and teach me" (Ps. 25:4-5). Let's pray that prayer together right now!

Then we learn about Jesus by studying our Bibles. The Bible can look like such a big book! But the Lord lets us learn things just like we learn them at school: a little at a time. After all, you don't learn your multiplication tables in the first grade! You start with counting, then adding and subtracting . . . and by the time you're a little older, you're ready for multiplication tables! Isaiah says we learn God's Word "line by line, rule by rule, here a little and there a little" (Isa. 28:13). The Bible also tells us to study God's Word so that we will have the tools we need to live for the Lord (2 Tim. 2:15).

We also learn from watching other believers. Paul told the people he taught to do the things they saw him do (Phil. 4:9). And Isaiah tells us that as we gather in the house of the Lord, "He will teach us His ways, and we will walk in His paths."

Finally, the Lord promises to teach us. The Lord says that He will teach us the way we should go (Ps. 32:8). Later, Jesus told His disciples to learn from Him (Matt. 11:29) and promised that the Holy Spirit would help teach them (John 14:26).

The Lord promises us the same bread of life that He promised His disciples long ago. Let's not turn away like some of the people did. Let's keep growing in Him and learning more about Him, so that bread can keep filling us up!

TO KILL A MOCKINGBIRD
The Silver Sword
ROBINSON CRUSOE
HAWAII
Churchill
Churchill
Churchill
ALASKA
David Livingstone
LOS ANGELES
John Wesley's Journal
Arabian Nights
BIBLE
West from Home
HAYFORD'S BIBLE HANDBOOK
Word Finder
Pilgrim's Progress
Hymnal
Huckleberry Finn
Tom Sawyer
Western Civilization Vol. I
Through the Fire Without Burning
Snow Treasure
POPULAR CHILDREN'S POETRY
STRONG'S CONCORDANCE
ATLAS

More About Jesus

Eliza E. Hewitt
John R. Sweney
1. More a - bout Je - sus would I know, More of His grace to oth - ers show; More of His sav - ing full - ness see, More of His love who died for me.
2. More a - bout Je - sus let me learn, More of His ho - ly will dis - cern; Spir - it of God, my Teach - er be, Show - ing the things of Christ to me.
3. More a - bout Je - sus in His Word, Hold - ing com - mun - ion with my Lord; Hear - ing His voice in ev - 'ry line, Mak - ing each faith - ful say - ing mine.
4. More a - bout Je - sus on His throne, Rich - es in glo - ry all His own; More of His king - dom's sure in - crease; More of His com - ing, Prince of Peace.
Refrain
More, more a - bout Je - sus, More, more a - bout Je - sus; More of His sav - ing full - ness see, More of His love who died for me.

I've always told my children that just like Mom and Dad have jobs that they have to do every day, kids have a job too. Their job is growing up. That may sound like an easy job, because you don't have to do anything for your body to grow! But there are other things to learn while you're growing up . . . and you won't grow to be a capable adult if you don't learn all of the parts of the growing-up-kid job!

Some of a kid's job is to go to school; some of it is learning how to get along with all different kinds of people. Other parts are learning responsibility, learning to hear God's voice, and learning to share. But one part—a very *big* part—is learning to obey. Right now, you're learning to obey your parents and teachers, but you learn to obey now so that as you grow, you will know how to obey God when He speaks to you.

Whether you're obeying your parents, your teachers, or the Lord, obedience takes place in two ways—in action and in attitude. Sometimes you may *do* what you're told, but on the inside you're really angry about having to do it. Or you may intend to obey, but you grow forgetful or lazy and don't get the job done. Either way, it's only obeying halfway. We need to get our actions and our attitudes to match up!

Obeying with our actions can sometimes be the easier of the two to learn because we can see it. Either we've done something or we haven't. But the Bible says that while people look at the outward appearance (our actions), God looks at our hearts (1 Sam. 16:7). He knows if our actions and attitudes are matching up! That's where trust comes in. Sometimes we don't "match up" because we aren't trusting the person we're obeying.

One day, when I was a little girl, I came home with my Weekly Reader Book Order Form. Of course, there was a whole set of Winnie the Pooh books I wanted to get. But to my surprise, my parents said no, I couldn't get those books. Boy, was I mad! I obeyed all right, but my attitude wasn't very trustful. I just knew they didn't understand how much I wanted those books and was sure they didn't care either. I stayed mad for weeks until Christmas Day rolled around . . . and guess what was under the Christmas tree for me. The Winnie the Pooh books! I had obeyed in action, but I didn't trust that my parents were looking out for my best interests. I also spent a miserable couple of weeks feeling sorry for myself and being angry with my mom and dad.

We can do the same thing with the Lord. We can obey with our actions, but be angry and afraid in our attitudes. The song, "Trust and Obey," was written following a service where a young man had given his testimony. As he was talking, he said that he didn't understand all of the things going on in his life. Rather than being upset over them, though, he said he was going to trust and obey God anyway! Having heard that testimony, John Sammis wrote this song to remind us that the only way to true happiness in our lives with the Lord is to trust and obey Him! Take a minute and check your attitudes and actions. Is there a place where they need to match up so that you're trusting and obeying Jesus?

Trust and Obey

John H. Sammis — Daniel B. Towner

1. When we walk with the Lord in the light of His
2. Not a shad - ow can rise, not a cloud in the
3. Not a bur - den we bear, not a sor - row we
4. But we nev - er can prove the de - lights of His
5. Then in fel - low - ship sweet we will sit at His

Word, What a glo - ry He sheds on our way!
skies, But His smile quick - ly drives it a - way;
share, But our toil He doth rich - ly re - pay;
love Un - til all on the al - tar we lay;
feet, Or we'll walk by His side in the way;

While we do His good will He a - bides with us
Not a doubt nor a fear, not a sigh nor a
Not a grief nor a loss, not a frown nor a
For the fa - vor He shows and the joy he be -
What He says we will do, where He sends we will

still, And with all who will
tear, Can a - bide while we
cross, But is blest if we trust and o - bey.
stows Are for them who will
go, Nev - er fear, on - ly

Refrain

Trust and o - bey, for there's no oth - er way To be

hap - py in Je - sus, But to trust and o - bey.

Have you ever heard the old "School Days" song? You know, the one that talks about learning "readin'," "writin'," and " 'rithmetic." Sometimes people call it learning "the three R's," even though you have to play with the spelling to get them all to begin with "R"! Instead of the three R's, though, I want to talk about God's *five* R's for excellence. God loves you so much that He wants to see you reach for the highest and best you can be for His glory. To top it off, God has a plan for your life—it's exciting and designed just for *you*!

The first "R" is *Respond* to God's call. God is ready and willing to talk to any of His children and lead them in the path He has for them. "It isn't that I've already accomplished the goal or that I am already perfect; but I continue to push forward so that I may grasp the purpose that God has for *me*!" (Phil. 3:12)

Recognize that you can't do it alone is the second "R." We have to run the race before us, looking to Jesus for our strength because He is the One who began our faith and He is the One who will complete it (Heb. 12:1-2). Jesus is called the "Beginning and the End" (Rev. 1:8). And it's great to know that no matter where we are in answering God's call on our lives, He's right there with us.

The next "R" is *Reach* for the next level. Because God wants us to become everything we can be, He requires growth of us. We can never be content to stay the way we are, but should constantly be asking the Lord to help us become more like Him. "I do not think that I have reached my highest level of achievement; but one thing I will do: I leave behind the things that I've already accomplished and reach forward to those things which are ahead" (Phil. 3:13).

Fourth, we need to *Require* excellence of ourselves. This doesn't mean that we are to be in competition with everyone else. It *does* mean that we should always do our personal best. After all, we are doing it for Jesus! "Don't you know that those who run in a race all run, but only one receives the prize? So run in such a way that you may obtain it" (1 Cor. 9:24).

The last "R" is *Remain* focused on the "prize." We are told to "press toward the goal for the prize of the *upward call* of God in Christ Jesus" (Phil. 3:14). The prize is the joy of obeying Jesus' call!

Where do you need to move to the next level? Maybe you need to learn your multiplication tables. Maybe you need to start reading your Bible every day. Maybe you need to start showing more kindness or patience or joy. Whatever it is, the Lord is calling you to take His hand and step up!

An apple a day keeps the doctor away...

Higher Ground

Johnson Oatman, Jr. — Charles H. Gabriel

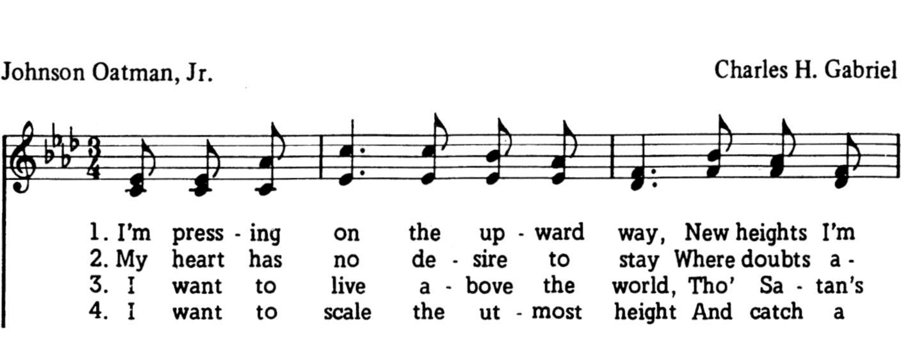
1. I'm pressing on the upward way, New heights I'm
2. My heart has no desire to stay Where doubts a-
3. I want to live above the world, Tho' Satan's
4. I want to scale the utmost height And catch a

gaining ev'ry day; Still praying as I'm onward
rise and fears dismay; Tho' some may dwell where these a-
darts at me are hurled; For faith has caught the joyful
gleam of glory bright; But still I'll pray till Heav'n I've

Refrain
bound, "Lord, plant my feet on higher ground."
bound, My prayer, my aim is higher ground.
sound, The song of saints on higher ground.
found, "Lord, lead me on to higher ground."
Lord, lift me

up and let me stand, By faith, on Heaven's tableland, A higher

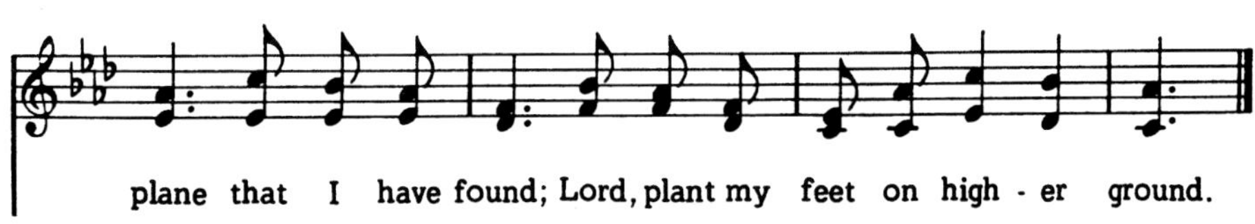
plane that I have found; Lord, plant my feet on higher ground.

Did you know that there is a difference between being a believer in Jesus and a disciple of Jesus? "Believers" take God at His Word and accept His gift of salvation in Jesus. They believe that Jesus is the Son of God. They love Him. Jesus lives in their hearts now and they expect to spend all of eternity with Him in heaven. That's a good thing! If you're going to be a disciple, you do that too. But a "disciple" is a person who not only lets Jesus change them on the inside, but also lets Him change them on the outside.

In Jesus' time, there were many people who believed: the 5,000 people who ate from the five loaves and two fishes believed (John 6:5-14); the many people Jesus healed believed (Matt. 12:15); the people who sang before Him as He entered Jerusalem on Palm Sunday believed in Him (Luke 19:28-40). But those people didn't follow Him. Even demons believe in God and tremble! (James 2:19) And we *know* they don't follow Jesus!

The Bible tells us about some others who chose not to follow Jesus. Some people were afraid to follow (John 7:13; 9:22). They were afraid that the Pharisees would punish them or people would reject them if they followed Jesus. The Apostle Matthew tells how Jesus asked a young man to leave everything and follow Him. But the young man didn't want to give up his possessions. The Bible says the young man "went away filled with sadness" (Matt. 19:16-22). He was sad not to follow Jesus—obviously he believed that Jesus was the Savior—but he was unwilling to give up everything for Jesus. There were things in his life that were more important to him than Jesus.

There is another group of people who *did* follow Jesus (4:19-22). Can you imagine being at your job and suddenly one day, Someone walks up and says, "Will you follow Me?" That's what happened to some fishermen named Peter, Andrew, James, and John when they encountered Jesus. The Bible says they *immediately* left their nets and followed Jesus. These are some of the men who became Jesus' disciples in the Bible. They are the people who knew Jesus most closely. They spent every day with Him, ate their meals with Him, and talked everything over with Him. He was their Teacher and Friend, as well as their Savior.

Jesus asks the same thing of us today. He wants each one of us to go *beyond* just believing in Him and become His disciple. He wants us to become more and more like Him. The Bible teaches us to "become followers of God—just like children are followers of their parents" (Eph. 5:1), and the Apostle Paul challenges us to have "the mind of Christ"—learning to think about things like Jesus does (1 Cor. 2:16).

We won't walk the hills of Judea with Jesus like the first disciples did, but we can talk to Him through prayer and learn about Him through reading and studying our Bibles. The Holy Spirit will guide us into all truth so that we can know more about Jesus (John 16:13). As we learn those things and draw closer to Jesus, He will become more than our Savior; He will become our Teacher and Friend!

Lead On, O King Eternal

Ernest W. Shurtleff | Henry T. Smart

1. Lead on, O King E - ter - nal, The day of march has come;
2. Lead on, O King E - ter - nal, Till sin's fierce war shall cease,
3. Lead on, O King E - ter - nal, We fol - low, not with fears;
Hence-forth in fields of con-quest Your tents shall be our home,
And ho - li - ness shall whis-per The sweet A - men of peace;
For glad-ness breaks like morn - ing Wher - e'er Your face ap - pears;
Through days of prep - a - ra - tion Your grace has made us strong,
For not with swords loud clash - ing, Nor roll of stir - ring drums,
Your cross is lift - ed o'er us; We jour-ney in its light:
And now, O King E - ter - nal, We lift our bat - tle song.
With deeds of love and mer - cy The heav'n-ly king-dom comes.
The crown a-waits the con-quest; Lead on, O God of might. A-men.

October : Honoring the King

When Jack Hayford was fourteen years old, he sat in a church service where the speaker was telling the stories of how some hymns had come to be written. Jack was impressed with the fact that these men and women had written something that was still blessing the church of Jesus long after they had died. "How I would love someday to write something like that!" thought Jack. "I would like to write a song that would outlive me and still be sung all around the world by God's people!" God granted that desire of Jack's heart through several songs. But none of his songs have been sung more than "Majesty."

Jack and his wife, Anna, were on vacation in England the year that nation was celebrating the 25th anniversary of Queen Elizabeth's coronation. Every person they met seemed to be filled with a sense of rejoicing in their ruler. That rejoicing also seemed to provide a sense of history and dignity that became the background for everything that was happening as the nation prepared for its celebration.

One day, Jack and Anna drove out to see the home of Winston Churchill, who was England's Prime Minister during the desperate days of World War II. Mr. Churchill had inspired a nation to stand firm in the face of a vicious army that outnumbered theirs and had more advanced weapons than they did. He became one of the great people of history in our century and a man of destiny for his nation.

As Jack and Anna walked through this beautiful palace that had been given to the Churchill family by Queen Anne 200 years earlier, Jack began thinking about Mr. Churchill's remarkable life. "Being raised in a beautiful and royal environment like this would *have* to make a person believe that they were a person of destiny—someone who would make a difference!" he said to his wife.

All of a sudden, he began to think about the kind of royal atmosphere our King Jesus has allowed us to live in! Through our acceptance of Jesus as our Savior, He has opened up a life full of purpose, destiny, and royalty for *us*! Jesus is seated in heavenly places and has given us the same power that He used to conquer Satan (Eph. 1:19-22; 2:6). He wants us to be people who make a difference in the world around us through prayer, through sharing the Good News of Jesus, and through living the kind of life He wants us to live.

Jack and Anna walked back to their car. As they drove away, he asked Anna to write down some words. They were the words to "Majesty."

God is calling you to be a person of destiny. Ask Him to put into your heart desires that He will fulfill as you grow up. The Bible says, "If you seek God's kingdom and what He wants first, all these other things that you desire will be given to you" (Matt. 6:33). Just as surely as God answered young Jack Hayford's desire to "write a song that outlived him," He will fulfill desires in your heart and cause you to become a young man or a young woman who makes a difference!

Majesty
JWH
Jack W. Hayford
Maj - es - ty, worship His Maj - es - ty. Un - to
Je - sus be all glo - ry, hon - or, and praise.
Maj - es - ty, king-dom au - thor - i - ty flows from His
throne un - to His own; His an - them raise. So ex -
alt, lift up on high the name of Je - sus. Mag - ni -
fy, come glo - ri - fy Christ Je - sus, the King.
Maj - es - ty, wor - ship His Maj - es - ty; Je - sus who
died, now glo - ri - fied, King of all kings.
© Copyright 1981 Rocksmith Music, c/o Trust Management, Inc., P.O. Box 9526, Calabasas, CA 91372
All rights reserved. Used by permission.

When we think of worship, Hallelujah! we usually think only of giving praise to God . . . and that is an important part of worship. But the word means much more than that. It actually means to place full and correct value on the thing or person you are worshiping. So when we worship the Lord, many things are going on: we are giving Him praise for how great He is, we are thanking Him for the many wonderful things He has done for us, we are saying how much He is *worth* to us, we are admitting that without Him we would have nothing and be nothing, we are placing Him in His rightful place as our King, and we are telling Him how much we love Him. All of those things go into worshiping God!

The song, "O Worship the King," was written by a man who understood all of those features of worship. His name was Sir Robert Grant. During his lifetime, Robert was a very important man. He served in the Parliament in England (that would be like being a Senator in our country) during the reign of King George IV. Later, during the reign of King William IV, he was the Governor over Bombay, when England ruled over India. But Robert recognized that he owed allegiance to an even higher King! The Bible tells us that Jesus is the "King of kings" (Rev. 17:14), and Robert loved and served Jesus first of all. In his song, Robert lists six titles for the Lord to remind us of some of the things we are to worship Him for.

God is our *Shield.* That means that He protects us. He not only protects us from harm right now (Pss. 3:1-3; 91:1-2), but He gives us the shield of His salvation. That's eternal protection! (18:35)

The Ancient of Days doesn't describe something that God does for us, it tells us something that God is: He is eternal, faithful, changeless. We can build our lives on Him because He is the same yesterday, today, and always (Mal. 3:6; Heb. 13:8; James 1:17).

Maker is another word for "creator." The Bible says that everything we have comes from the Lord starting with the ability to take each breath! (Acts 17:25) He knows how many hairs are on our heads (Matt. 10:30). He knows each step that we take (Ps. 37:23). The Bible also says that the Lord knows what is going to happen in each of our days (139:16).

A *Defender* is someone who fights for you. We don't have to fight our own battles because we are never alone, and the Lord has promised to fight our battles for us (Ex. 14:14; Ps. 62:2, 6).

As our *Redeemer* (another word for savior), Jesus fought the biggest battle for us: the battle against the devil, sin, and death. We know the end of the story! Jesus won! The prize He was fighting for was *us,* so He not only beat the devil, but He won us! (Ps. 103:4; Gal. 3:13; Titus 2:14)

Then, our King doesn't just think of us as people for Him to rule over. He also wants to be our *Friend* (Prov. 18:24; John 15:15).

As you worship our King Jesus today, what do you want to thank Him for? Has He shown Himself to be your Shield and Defender? Or do you want to simply thank Him for being your Creator or Friend? Whichever title you choose to thank Him for, give our King praise today!

O Worship The King
Sir Robert H. Grant
Johann M. Haydn
1. O wor - ship the King, all glo - rious a - bove, O
2. O tell of His might, O sing of His grace, Whose
3. Thy boun - ti - ful care what tongue can re - cite? It
4. Frail chil - dren of dust, and fee - ble as frail, In
grate - ful - ly sing His pow'r and His love; Our
robe is the light, whose can - o - py space. His
breathes in the air, it shines in the light; It
Thee do we trust, nor find Thee to fail; Thy
Shield and De - fend - er, the An - cient of Days, Pa -
char - iots of wrath the deep thun - der clouds form, And
streams from the hills, it de - scends to the plain, And
mer - cies how ten - der! How firm to the end! Our
vil - ioned in splen - dor and gird - ed with praise.
dark is His path on the wings of the storm.
sweet - ly dis - tills in the dew and the rain.
Mak - er, De - fend - er, Re - deem - er and Friend. A - men.

Nero was the most wicked of all the Roman emperors. He killed anyone who challenged his authority, including his wife and his mother. He destroyed large areas of Rome so that he could rebuild them to look the way he wanted them to, regardless of the loss it caused to other people. He also viciously persecuted Christians, killing them in large numbers. His evil was so unthinkable, and his life so hardened against God and people, that historians tell us he used the bodies of Christian martyrs as torches to light his gardens. He was a wicked and cruel man to have as a king.

It was during Nero's rule that the Apostle Paul was thrown into prison in Rome, where he spent the rest of his life. While he was in prison, however, Paul wrote many of the books of the Bible that we now have in the New Testament. In his letter to the Philippians, Paul writes from his prison cell, "Rejoice in the Lord always. Again I will say, rejoice!" (Phil. 4:4)

How could Paul write something like that to other believers when they had such a cruel king who was seeking to destroy their lives? How could Paul believe that when he was stuck in prison? We find the answer to those questions in another one of Paul's letters. When he wrote to the Corinthians, Paul said that if you become a Christian while you are a slave, you are living in the Lord's freedom! If you become a Christian when you are free, you become the Lord's slave! (1 Cor. 7:22) In another place Paul calls himself the Lord's prisoner (Eph. 4:1). Paul was willing to always be serving the Lord because He is the very best of Kings! So even though Paul was the prisoner of an earthly king in Rome when he wrote those words, he knew that he had found freedom in his spirit. The things that people tried to do to him couldn't hold Paul's spirit prisoner. In the middle of terrible circumstances he was still serving His true, heavenly King. That's why he could keep rejoicing!

This wasn't the first time Paul had worshiped in a jail cell, either. Paul and Silas were worshiping the Lord by singing songs of praise in the middle of the night! In this case, their praise brought several people to salvation, including the jail keeper! (Acts 16:22-34)

Honoring our King doesn't depend on our circumstances. In fact, after Paul tells the Philippians to rejoice, he says, "I've learned to be content no matter what is happening to me. I've had times of great need and times of great provision. I've had times when I've been very hungry, and times when I've been very full" (Phil. 4:11-12). How could he do that? Because Paul recognized that God is always worthy of worship!

What does your day hold that may be unpleasant? It can't hold your spirit prisoner any more than a jail cell could hold Paul's! I guarantee that if you will worship God Hallelujah! in the middle of it, He will meet you right where you are. Besides, if Paul could worship the Lord in prison, I guess I can worship God in the middle of what's happening to me! How about you?

Rejoice, the Lord Is King
Charles Wesley
John Darwall
1. Re - joice, the Lord is King; Your Lord and King a - dore! Re - joice, give
2. Je - sus, the Sav-iour, reigns, The God of truth and love; When He had
3. His king-dom can-not fail; He rules o'er earth and heaven; The keys of
4. Re - joice in glor-ious hope! Our Lord, the Judge, shall come, And take His
thanks, and sing, And tri-umph ev - er - more. Lift up your heart,
purged our stains, He took His seat a - bove. Lift up your heart,
death and hell Are to our Je - sus given. Lift up your heart,
ser - vants up to their e - ter - nal home. Lift up your heart,
lift up your voice! Re - joice, a - gain I say, re - - joice!
lift up your voice! Re - joice, a - gain I say, re - - joice!
lift up your voice! Re - joice, a - gain I say, re - - joice!
lift up your voice! Re - joice, a - gain I say, re - - joice! A-men.

The Bible says that we are to live like people who "see" invisible things (2 Cor. 4:18). The Bible says that God dwells in "secret places" (Ps. 18:11). God is even described as the invisible God (1 Tim. 1:17). All of this invisible stuff can sound kind of spooky, like God is going to try to sneak up on us! But have you ever thought about the things that are invisible in our lives, and we don't think anything strange about it?

How about planting a garden? We put seeds in the ground and expect plants to come up. It takes awhile before the seedlings pop up through the ground. But eventually they do, and what was invisible becomes visible. We simply believe that growth is happening.

Do you have electricity in your house? Of course you do. But you can't see it! You only see what it does. It runs the lights; it runs the TV; it may even run your family's stove. You simply trust that when you flip the switch, the power will be there to make the lights come on.

In the same way, God is always working in our lives, in our hearts, and in the situations we face every day. Sometimes we don't see Him doing anything, but He is always working—causing us to grow and working in us by His power.

Most of what God does in our lives is invisible at first. He starts by drawing us to Jesus and working in our hearts so that we want to ask Jesus to come and live in us. We don't see it happening . . . it's invisible! But one day we come to a point of asking Jesus into our hearts and our lives change. Then what was invisible (God working in our hearts) becomes visible.

Our faith is invisible too. We believe God is there, and we believe what He's told us, though we can't see it or touch it. Yet God promised that He will answer us and that He will be with us. He also says that our faith is a powerful force. Our faith (the invisible) is mighty enough to move mountains (Mark 11:22-23).

Another invisible thing that God does in our lives is make us like Him. God makes all things beautiful in time (Ecc. 3:11). But a lot of what happens to make things beautiful in us is invisible to us. Just like the garden, it sometimes takes awhile before we see things growing. But the Lord promises that He will cause the fruit of the Spirit to grow in our lives: love, joy, peace, patience, kindness, goodness, faithfulness, gentleness, and self-control (Gal. 5:22-23). Sometimes we don't see Him growing that fruit until one day, all of a sudden, it just seems to sprout out, and His invisible work become visible!

Don't be discouraged when you don't see things happening. Just keep your eyes open and you'll soon see the invisible becoming visible! Our God, who is invisible, is always working in the invisible places of our hearts!

Immortal, Invisible, God Only Wise
Walter Chalmers Smith
From J. Roberts' Canaidauy Cyssegr
1. Im - mor - tal, in - vis - i - ble, God on - ly wise,
2. Un - rest - ing, un - hast - ing, and si - lent as light,
3. To all, life Thou giv - est, to both great and small,
4. Great Fa - ther of glo - ry, pure Fa - ther of light,
In light in - ac - ces - si - ble hid from our eyes,
Nor want - ing, nor wast - ing, Thou rul - est in might;
In all life Thou liv - est, the true life of all;
Thine an - gels a - dore Thee, all veil - ing their sight;
Most bless - ed, most glo - rious, the An - cient of Days,
Thy jus - tice like moun - tains high soar - ing a - bove
We blos - som and flour - ish as leaves on the tree,
All praise we would ren - der; O help us to see
Al - might - y, vic - to - rious, Thy great name we praise!
Thy clouds, which are foun - tains of good - ness and love.
And with - er and per - ish – but nought chang - eth Thee.
'Tis on - ly the splen - dor of light hid - eth Thee!

What makes a person great? Some people think it's being in a high position and being in charge. Some people think it's being famous. What do you think makes a person great?

The Bible tells us about a time when the disciples argued over this. They each wanted to be an important person when Jesus set up His kingdom; so Jesus had to teach them a lesson. He taught them, "If anyone wants to be the most important, then he should *serve* everyone" (Mark 9:35).

What makes us great is that we serve one another . . . but even before that can happen, we are supposed to become God's servants (Rom. 6:22). So how do we serve the Lord? Well, there are a lot of answers to that: we can do kind things for people; we can tell people about the Lord; and we can obey God's commands. But the first and most important way that we serve the Lord is by giving Him praise (Ps. 100:2). That's how we tell the Lord how much we love Him—no matter what's happening around us!

I learned that in a kind of interesting way. On January 17, 1994, there was a huge earthquake where I live. Have you ever been in an earthquake? I had been in other ones, and they weren't that scary to me . . . but this one was! First of all it happened at night and made all the power in the city go out, so it was really dark. I couldn't even see my hand when I held it up in front of my face! Then, it was huge! When I woke up, my bed was bouncing up and down about twelve inches off the floor. Of course, I was worried about my children, but we all got together really fast, so I knew they were OK. But that night, we sat in the dark together with the ground bouncing us up and down, and all we could hear was the sound of glass breaking all over the house.

Well, once it got light, you can imagine what the inside of our house looked like! Every cupboard in the kitchen had come open and things had come flying out and broken all over the floor. All the books had come out of the bookcases. The fish aquarium had broken so there was water and glass all over the family room, and the poor fish didn't stand a chance. Every room had broken things in it. What a job to clean up! And there was no electricity so there was no vacuum to use! We spent the whole day cleaning up. And in the middle of that awful, scary, messy day, I found myself singing the song, "I Was Made for You" over and over again.

I realized in a new way that no matter what *things* were suddenly taken away, or what kind of a scary situation I found myself in, I was going to praise the Lord anyway, because the most important thing in my life is that I belong to Him and serve Him. As we praise the Lord and tell Him how much we love Him, the love He has put in our hearts can grow and grow! Pretty soon, our hearts will be so full of love that it will spill over onto everyone around us!

Praise the Lord—no matter what's happening! Let His love in your heart keep growing! And you'll see that having Jesus with you will make everything else easier to handle!

I Was Made to Praise You

CC
Chris Christensen
I ___ was made to praise ___ You, I ___ was made to
I ___ will al - ways praise ___ You, I ___ will al - ways
glo - ri - fy Your ___ name in ev - 'ry cir - cum - stance, to find a
glo - ri - fy Your ___ name in ev - 'ry cir - cum - stance, I'll find a
chance to thank You. ___ I was made to love ___ You,
chance to thank You. ___ I will al - ways love ___ You,
I ___ was made to wor - ship at Your feet and to o -
I ___ will al - ways wor - ship at Your feet and I'll o -
bey You, Lord, I was made for You.
bey You, Lord, I was made for You.

The Bible says that if *we* don't praise the Lord, the rocks will cry out in praise to God! But sometimes when it's time to give the Lord praise, it's hard to think of things to praise Him for! Has that ever happened to you? It's happened to me. If you're running short on things to praise the Lord for, you can read through this song for some ideas. And here are also some reasons from Scripture to help get you going!

He helps us (Ps. 28:7; Isa. 41:10) • He is good (Pss. 54:6; 135:3) • He gives us truth (Ps. 138:2; Deut. 32:4) • For the beauty of creation (Pss. 8:3; 19:1) • He has made our bodies wonderfully (Ps. 139:14) • He heals us (Pss. 103:3; 147:3) • He provides everything we need (Phil. 4:19) • We are His people (Ps. 95:7; 1 Peter 2:9) • His works toward us are wonderful (Pss. 26:7; 107:31) • The Lord is compassionate toward us (Ps. 111:4) • He is our God (Ps. 118:28) • He made the day and the night (Gen. 1:4-5; Jer. 33:20) • He gives us breath (Acts 17:25) • He gives us food (Ps. 111:5) • He never breaks His promises (1 Kings 8:56; Ps. 56:10) • He sent Jesus (John 3:16) • He makes all things beautiful (Ecc. 3:11) • He plans for our future (Ps. 139:16; Jer. 29:11) • His mercies are new each day (Lam. 3:22) • He guides us (Prov. 3:6) • He forgives us (1 John 1:9) • He hears us (Pss. 34:17; 118:21) • He gives us abundant life (John 10:10) • He promises to remove sorrow and replace it with joy (Isa. 61:3) • We will spend eternity with Him (1 Thes. 4:17) • He placed us in our family (Gal. 3:26)• He loves us with an everlasting love (Jer. 31:3) • He conquered sin and death for us (Matt. 26:28; 1 Tim. 1:10) • He gives us peace (John 14:27; Phil. 4:7) • He is always with us (Heb. 13:5) • He comforts us (Ps. 71:21; Isa. 40:1-2) • He gives us hope (Rom. 15:4; 1 Cor. 13:13) • He gives us His Word (Ps. 107:20; 2 Tim. 3:16) • Our church (Acts 12:12; Gal. 6:2; Heb. 10:25) • He makes us more like Him (2 Cor. 3:18) • He gives us rain (Ps. 65:9-10) • He fills us with His Spirit (Eph. 3:19; 5:18) • He completes what He begins in us (Phil. 1:6) • We're not alone in hard times (Ps. 91:4; 1 Cor. 10:13)

Can you think of more? Add them to the list and then praise the Lord as you sing: "To God be the glory, *great* things He has done!"

To God Be The Glory

Fanny J. Crosby — William H. Doane

1. To God be the glo - ry, great things He hath done, So
2. O per - fect re - dem - tion, the pur - chase of blood! To
3. Great things He hath taught us, great things He hath done, And
loved He the world that He gave us His Son, Who
ev - 'ry be - liev - er the prom - ise of God; The
great our re - joic - ing thro' Je - sus the Son; But
yield - ed His life an a - tone - ment for sin, And
vil - est of - fend - er who tru - ly be - lieves, That
pur - er and high - er and great - er will be Our
o - pened the Life - gate that all may go in.
mo - ment from Je - sus a par - don re - ceives.
won - der, our trans - port, when Je - sus we see.
Refrain
Praise the Lord, praise the Lord, Let the earth hear His voice! Praise the
Lord, praise the Lord, Let the peo - ple re - joice! O
come to the Fa - ther thro' Je - sus the Son, And
give Him the glo - ry, great things He hath done.

It seems like everywhere we go these days, we hear a lot of discussion on how human beings should take care of the earth. We hear that we should recycle bottles, cans, and paper to cut down on what goes into the dumps. We hear about how we should or shouldn't use certain products so that we can take better care of the ozone layer. People on the news talk about endangered species, the rainforest, and global warming. They're worried that we have treated our world in such a careless way that we are actually destroying it! There are even some people who think that the care of the earth is so important, they've made it more important than the Lord. And when something in someone's life is more important than the Lord, then that thing has become their god. There are other people who place more value on saving the endangered animals than they do on making things better for people.

So, what are we supposed to do about the earth? And more importantly, how does the Bible say we're supposed to think about the earth? God gave His first command to people about the earth: He wanted us to govern the earth, to control it, and to make it be the most it could be—the most beautiful, the most productive. God wanted us to be managers of the earth! (Gen. 1:28) The problem, of course, is that when sin came, the earth was affected too. But what God said is still the same: we need to take care of the earth, not because we worship it and not because we value it above people but because God commanded it! It might also help us take better care of the earth if we understood what the Lord wants us to use it for!

First, the Lord wants us simply to enjoy it! Our earth is beautiful and God made it just for us. The Bible says that the Lord "gives us all things to enjoy" (1 Tim. 6:17). The Old Testament talks about the land that the Lord gave the Children of Israel. He tells them that when the battles were all over, they were to go to their own part of the land and just "enjoy it"! (Josh. 1:15)

Then, the Lord gave us the earth to provide food for us. The Lord makes grass grow to feed the animals and plants to feed people "that he may bring forth food from the earth" (Ps. 104:14). "The earth is full of the goodness of the Lord" (33:5). The Lord "crowns the year with goodness" and gives us great abundance (65:11).

The Lord also gave us the earth to encourage us to praise Him! The Apostle Paul writes that through creation *every person* has a testimony of God (Rom. 1:18-23). David, in awe, sang before the Lord, "When I look at the heavens, the work of Your fingers, and the beauty of the moon and stars, it's a mystery to me that You pay any attention to people" (Ps. 8:3-4). But, thank the Lord, He does! And He has shown us the great value He places on us through the beautiful world He has made for us. He gave us our earth to take care of, but first, like the Prophet Isaiah wrote, let's "be glad and give praise for what God has created" (Isa. 65:18).

I Sing the Mighty Power of God

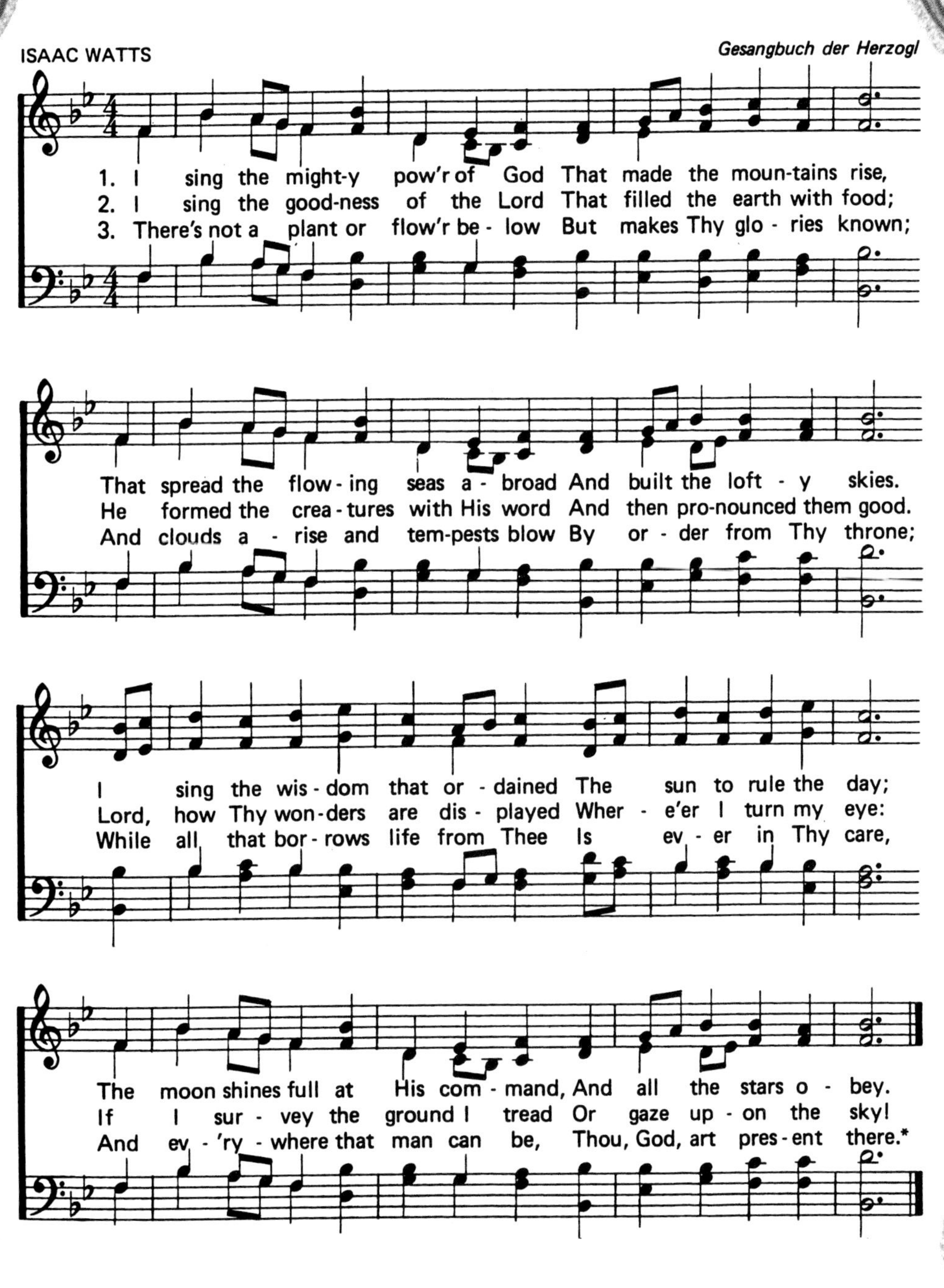

ISAAC WATTS
Gesangbuch der Herzogl
1. I sing the might-y pow'r of God That made the moun-tains rise,
2. I sing the good-ness of the Lord That filled the earth with food;
3. There's not a plant or flow'r be - low But makes Thy glo - ries known;
That spread the flow - ing seas a - broad And built the loft - y skies.
He formed the crea - tures with His word And then pro-nounced them good.
And clouds a - rise and tem-pests blow By or - der from Thy throne;
I sing the wis - dom that or - dained The sun to rule the day;
Lord, how Thy won-ders are dis - played Wher - e'er I turn my eye:
While all that bor - rows life from Thee Is ev - er in Thy care,
The moon shines full at His com - mand, And all the stars o - bey.
If I sur - vey the ground I tread Or gaze up - on the sky!
And ev - 'ry - where that man can be, Thou, God, art pres - ent there.*

Henry Alford was a dedicated follower of Jesus Christ from the time he was a young man. At the age of sixteen, he wrote in the front of his Bible these words: "I do this day, in the presence of God and my own soul, renew my covenant with God, and solemnly determine henceforth to become His, and to do His work as far as in me lies." He fulfilled that commitment to the Lord as a pastor, as a composer, and as a writer.

"Come, Ye Thankful People, Come"—Henry's most famous hymn—reminds us first to praise the Lord for His provision for our needs. But then he applies the idea of growing and harvesting crops to our lives. Henry uses Jesus' parable to describe how at the end of time, God will separate the wheat (those who believe in Jesus) from the weeds (those who don't believe in Jesus) in the final harvest, as He brings His people home to heaven! (Matt. 13) In the song, Henry wrote, "Lord of harvest, grant that *we*; wholesome grain and pure may be."

That phrase reminds me of another one of Jesus' parables that tells us how we can become that "pure and wholesome grain." Jesus tells a parable about the planting of God's Word in four different kinds of hearts. He described how some of the seed fell along the side of a road and was snatched away by birds. Some of the other seed fell on stony ground and started to sprout, but because the soil was shallow, the seedlings withered on the first hot day. Other seed fell into a weed patch, where the weeds shaded it from the sun and used up all the water. Those seeds didn't stand a chance. "But other seed fell on good ground and produced a crop" (Mark 4:1-9, 13-20).

Jesus then goes on to explain what the parable means. The ground along the wayside is like people who hear God's Word, but forget or ignore it so it can't change their lives. The stony ground describes people who are happy to receive God's Word but only want to obey it when the going is easy. The weed patch represents what Jesus called, "the cares of this world." Those are things that seem important at the moment, but they have no lasting value. People with that kind of ground in their hearts don't properly value the things of God. Then there are others who have "good ground" in their hearts. They receive the Word of God and it grows, and grows, and grows!

So how can we become the kind of field that Henry talked about? Anyone who's ever planted a garden knows that "good soil" takes a lot of work! We need to study and apply God's Word to our lives so that Satan can't steal away what God wants to do in us. We need to depend on God when hard things happen and not give up. After all, it's sometimes the severe weather that make plants' roots grow the deepest. Then weeding is a constant job in a garden, isn't it! We must make sure that we keep Jesus in "first place" in our lives.

As we do all of this, we become good soil in which the Lord can grow that wholesome and pure grain—ready for His use! That's something to be thankful for!

Come Ye Thankful People, Come

Henry Alford
George J. Elvey
1. Come, ye thank-ful peo - ple come, Raise the song of har - vest - home:
2. All the world is God's own field, Fruit un - to His praise to yield:
3. For the Lord our God shall come, And shall take His har - vest home:
4. E - ven so, Lord, quick - ly come To Thy fi - nal har - vest home:
All is safe - ly gath - ered in, Ere the win - ter storms be - gin.
Wheat and tares to - geth - er sown. Un - to joy or sor - row grown.
From His field shall in that day All of - fens - es purge a - way;
Gath - er Thou Thy peo - ple in, Free from sor - row, free from sin;
God, our Ma - ker, doth pro - vide For our wants to be sup - plied:
First the blade, and then the ear, Then the full corn shall ap - pear:
Give His an - gels charge at last In the fire the tares to cast,
There, for - ev - er pu - ri - fied, In Thy pres - ence to a - bide:
Come to God's own tem - ple, come, Raise the song of har - vest - home.
Lord of har - vest, grant that we Whole - some grain and pure may be.
But the fruit - ful ears to store In His gar - ner ev - er - more.
Come, with all Thine an - gels, come, Raise the glo - rious har - vest - home.

December: Christmas

Christmastime is filled with lots of things to go to: there are special church services (Candlelighting service is my favorite!), class parties, choir recitals, tree-trimming parties, caroling parties, Christmas plays, family dinners, maybe a party with your sports team, and, well . . . parties, parties, parties! How do you find out about all of these occasions? You receive an invitation, of course! So, along with receiving Christmas cards and Christmas presents, you usually receive some invitations too. But the only invitations that *really* matter are the "two invitations of Christmas." They're the invitations that make it possible for Jesus to spend Christmas at your house, and they are both talked about in the song, "O Come, All Ye Faithful."

The first invitation is the one God makes to us in the words, "O come, all ye faithful." The fact that Jesus came to earth in the first place was an invitation by God to come to Him. John 3:16 says that God *gave* His Son. All we have to do is believe—or accept the invitation He gives! In the Bible we see Jesus over and over again calling us to come: He invites us to come to Him (Matt. 11:28), to come and rest (Mark 6:31), to let children come to Him (10:14), to come and follow Him (Luke 18:22), to come and receive life (John 10:10), and to come and eat with Him (21:12). He wants to have us near Him! . . . But we have to want the same thing. The Bible also says that Jesus is standing at the door of our hearts asking, "Will you open the door and let Me come in?" All He's waiting for is for you to open the door of your heart! If you do, He promises, "I *will* come in" (Rev. 3:20).

The second invitation can be found in the words, "O come, let us adore Him." We make this invitation to the Lord through our worship and praise. The Bible says that our praise actually *invites* the Lord to come and be where we are! (Ps. 22:3) The Bible also tells us that though we were once separated from God by our sins (Eph. 2:12-14), now, through accepting Jesus' invitation, we can "draw near to God" (Heb. 10:22). Just think about this: accepting Jesus' invitation of salvation makes it possible for God to accept our invitation of worship! Once we have accepted Jesus' invitation, we can draw near to God and He can draw near to us with the same love and closeness you have with your mom or dad.

Have you accepted Jesus' invitation? If you haven't, why don't you do that today? Open the door of your heart and let Him in. If you *have* done that, why don't you worship Him today, inviting Him to come your house. You see, Jesus wants to spend Christmas with you!

O Come All Ye Faithful

Latin hymn
Trans. By Frederick Oakeley
ADESTE FIDELES
From Wade's Cantus Diversi
1. O come, all ye faith - ful, joy - ful and tri - um - phant,
2. Sing, choirs of an - gels, sing in ex - ul - ta - tion,
3. Yea Lord, we greet Thee, born this hap - py morn - ing,
Come ye, O come ye to Beth - le - hem;
Sing all ye bright hosts of heav'n a - bove;
Je - sus, to Thee be all glo - ry giv'n;
Come and be - hold Him, born the King of an - gels:
Glo - ry to God, all glo - ry in the high - est:
Word of the Fa - ther, now in flesh ap - pear - ing:
O come, let us a - dore Him, O come, let us a -
dore Him, O come, let us a - dore Him, Christ, the Lord.

Charles Wesley wrote "Hark, the Herald Angels Sing" during a time when very few Christmas songs were being written. About 100 years earlier, the Puritans had held such political power in England that they had Christmas carols abolished because they thought they were part of a worldly celebration. The Puritans thought that if the holiday wasn't going to be *only* about Jesus then nothing should be celebrated.

In a way, they were concerned about the same things we are today. When we look around, there doesn't seem to be very many people emphasizing Jesus at Christmas. Most people put the emphasis on Santa Claus and getting presents. But although leaving Jesus out of Christmas is a sad thing, it does give us an opportunity to make Christmas a testimony about God's love for all people. One of the best ways to do that is to let people see the joy Jesus brings into our lives!

God doesn't just want us to be holy (set apart for Him), He wants us to be happy *while* we're being holy! (Ps. 5:11; Isa. 35:10; Gal. 5:22) I think Jesus was happy, and we *know* He was holy. People wouldn't have wanted to be around Him if He wasn't happy, yet the Bible tells about huge crowds of people coming to see Jesus and wanting to be near Him.

One way we can share God's holiness *and* happiness is through music! Look at what Charles did with his song: In verse 1 he simply invites us to join the angels in praise for the gift of God's Son and what it accomplished—"God and sinners reconciled!" That means that we've been brought back into relationship with God!

But in verses 2 and 3, he blended together so many different Scriptures, that people can see all of God's plan. The song by itself is a testimony of God's love! Look at all of these Scripture verses!

2

Christ by highest heaven adored; (Rev. 5:11-12)
Christ, the everlasting Lord! (Isa. 9:6)
Late in time behold Him come, (Gal. 4:4)
Offspring of the virgin's womb. (Isa. 7:14)
Veiled in flesh the Godhead see; (Col. 2:9)
Hail th' incarnate Deity, (Col. 2:9; John 1:14)
Pleased as man with men to dwell, (John 1:14)
Jesus, our Emmanuel! (Isa. 7:14)

3

Hail, the heaven-born Prince of Peace! (Isa. 9:6)
Hail, the sun of Righteousness! (Mal. 4:2)
Light and life to all He brings, (John 14:6)
Ris'n with healing in His wings. (Mal. 4:2)
Mild He lays His glory by, (Phil. 2:6-7)
Born that man no more may die. (John 10:10)
Born to raise the sons of earth, (1 Cor. 6:14; 2 Cor. 4:14)
Born to give them second birth. (John 3:1-5)

As we celebrate this Christmas, let's show Jesus' love to those around us: through our music, through our celebration, through our commitment to Jesus, and through our joy!

Hark, the Herald Angels Sing

Felix Mendelssohn
Charles Wesley
Adapted by William H. Cummings
1. Hark, the her - ald an - gels sing, "Glo - ry to the new - born King;
2. Christ, by high - est heaven a - dored; Christ, the ev - er - last - ing Lord!
3. Hail, the heaven - born Prince of Peace! Hail, the Sun of Righteous - ness!
Peace on earth, and mer - cy mild, God and sin - ners rec - on - ciled!"
Late in time be - hold Him come, Off - spring of the vir - gin's womb.
Light and life to all He brings, Ris'n with heal - ing in His wings.
Joy - ful, all ye na - tions, rise, Join the tri - umph of the skies;
Veiled in flesh the God - head see; Hail th' in - car - nate De - i - ty,
Mild He lays His glo - ry by, Born that man no more may die.
With th' an - gelic host pro - claim, "Christ is born in Beth - le - hem!"
Pleased as man with men to dwell, Je - sus, our Em - man - u - el!
Born to raise the sons of earth, Born to give them se - cond birth.
Hark, the her - ald an - gels sing, "Glo - ry to the new - born King."

HAPPY BIRTHDAY TO YOU.

Who would have ever thought that it would be the shepherds who would receive the first announcement of Jesus' birth? Certainly not the shepherds! Shepherds back then would have belonged to a pretty rugged crowd. They had a very physically demanding job: they lived outside with the sheep for a large portion of the year, and they had to fight wild animals to protect their sheep. These men were strong and didn't take any "guff" from anybody! They didn't use the most refined language, they weren't very clean, and didn't have the most elegant manners. After all—the sheep didn't care! They were also probably very poor. Yet these were the men who were the first to hear about the birth of God's Son, and from *angels* no less!

The shepherds were also the first ones who had the privilege of coming to worship Jesus, and the first ones who had the honor of telling others about Him.

"When [the shepherds] had seen [Jesus], they told everyone about this child, and all who heard it were amazed at what the shepherds said to them" (Luke 2:17-18).

So, in spite of the fact that the shepherds were rough, uneducated, and poor men, God chose them!

Have you ever thought about how God might choose to use *you* someday? From the shepherds we can learn that you don't have to be super-smart, you don't have to be super-rich, and you don't have to have fine clothes or great manners or a wonderful job. You don't even have to be perfect. You just have to be willing to obey when God speaks to you! Just like the shepherds.

The man who wrote this song was a man kind of like the shepherds—rough and poor. His name was Nahum Tate and he had a rather sad life. It started out well enough in the home of a minister in Ireland. He went to good schools and became a famous poet. But by the time Nahum died he was an alcoholic, penniless, and living in a poorhouse. Yet in Nahum's heart there was an awareness of God, and he wrote this Christmas carol about God meeting people where they are. Maybe Nahum understood this better than anyone—that no matter how people may have failed in their lives, God still wants to meet them right where they are and draw them to His Son.

God wants to do the same thing with you too. He wants to meet you where you are. You don't have to wait until you're grown up for God to talk to you or use you (1 Tim. 4:12). He wants to do it now! God can use anyone—even shepherds, even Nahum, even you! He always wants to bring His people to the highest goal that He has for them—He can even start when they're kids! He will do that for you if you listen for His voice and obey Him . . . just like the shepherds!

While Shepherds Watched Their Flocks

Nahum Tate
George F. Handel
1. While shep-herds watched their flocks by night, All seat - ed on the
2. "Fear not," said he, for might-y dread Had seized their trou-bled
3. "To you, in Da-vid's town, this day Is born, of Da-vid's
4. "The heav'n-ly Babe you there shall find To hu-man view dis-
5. "All glo-ry be to God on high, And to the earth be
ground, The an-gel of the Lord came down, and
minds. "Glad tid-ings of great joy I bring To
line, The Sav-iour, who is Christ the Lord; And
played, All mean-ly wrapped in swath-ing bands, And
peace, Good-will hence-forth from heav'n to men Be-
glo-ry shone a-round, And glo-ry shone a-round.
you and all man-kind, To you and all man-kind.
this shall be the sign, And this shall be the sign:
in a man-ger laid, And in a man-ger laid.
gin and nev-er cease, Be-gin and nev-er cease!"

I just can't sing the song "Silent Night" without thinking of snow! First of all, snow kind of muffles sound, so if you're in snow, it really is quiet! This song was also written in "snow season" in the Alps where Father Joseph Mohr lived. Right before Christmas, the organ in the church he pastored had broken. So that his congregation would still have special music for the Christmas Eve service, he decided to write a song. His friend, Franz Gruber, wrote the music, and with just a guitar, they sang their new song for Christmas 1818.

But there's a third reason that I think of snow when I sing "Silent Night," and it's found in the third verse. It describes Jesus as "love's pure light" and that with His coming we now see "the dawn of redeeming grace." Jesus came to bring us the light that would show the way back to God.

What does that have to do with snow? Well, the way back to God comes through the forgiveness of sins. If we believe in Jesus, the Bible says that God *will* forgive us. No matter what we've done, no matter how stained our hearts have become through the disobedient and wrong things we've done, the Lord will forgive us and make us clean. In the New Testament, we read that if we confess, or admit to, our sins, God is faithful and will forgive us for our sins (1 John 1:9). In the Old Testament, the Prophet Isaiah described this ultimate act of forgiveness in this way:

> *"Come and let's think about this together," says the Lord. "Though your sins are like scarlet, they shall be as white as snow; though they are red like crimson, they shall be as wool" (Isa. 1:18).*

The Bible has some other things to say about snow.

It says that the snow is here on the earth at God's command (Job 37:6). Then a few verses later, the Lord tells Job about the "treasury of snow" (38:22). The value of snow can be seen in its beauty and in God's creativity that no two snowflakes are alike. But the *real* treasure we find in snow is the picture it gives us of what God wants to do in our lives through forgiveness.

Later, in the Psalms, David echoes Isaiah's words by praying, "Wash me, and I shall be whiter than snow." Imagine! *Whiter* than snow! That's how clean God can make us through Jesus "who rescues us through His blood, and gives us forgiveness of sins, according to the riches of His grace" (Eph. 1:7). So in the "treasure of snow" we actually have a picture of "the riches of God's grace"!

Next time you're out in the snow, thank God that He sent us His greatest treasure—Jesus and that through Jesus He makes us as white as snow!

Silent Night

Joseph Mohr
Franz Gruber

1. Si - lent night! Ho - ly night! All is calm, all is bright 'Round yon
2. Si - lent night! Ho - ly night! Shep-herds quake at the sight! Glo - ries
3. Si - lent night! Ho - ly night! Son of God, love's pure light! Ra - diant

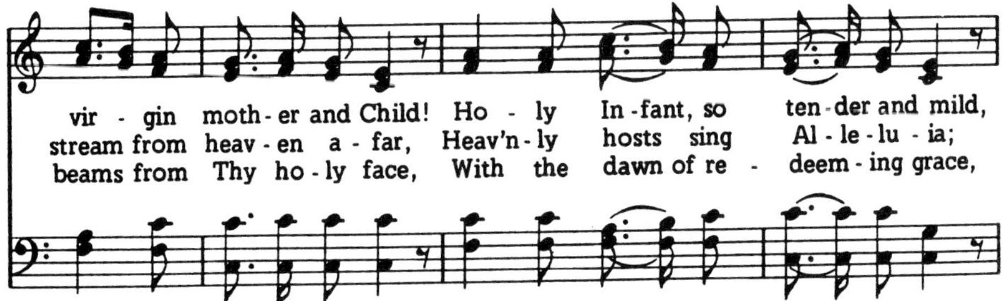
vir - gin moth - er and Child! Ho - ly In - fant, so ten - der and mild,
stream from heav - en a - far, Heav'n - ly hosts sing Al - le - lu - ia;
beams from Thy ho - ly face, With the dawn of re - deem - ing grace,

Sleep in heav - en - ly peace, Sleep in heav - en - ly peace.
Christ, the Sav - iour, is born, Christ, the Sav - iour, is born.
Je - sus, Lord, at Thy birth, Je - sus, Lord, at Thy birth.

January 1
Happy New Year!

January 11
Happy Birthday
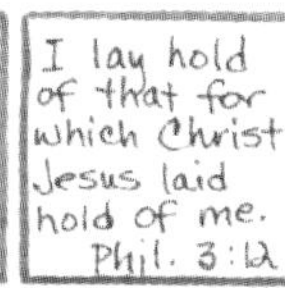
I lay hold of that for which Christ Jesus laid hold of me.
Phil. 3:12

February 14
Valentine's Day

President's Day

March 16
St. Patrick's Day

March 21
First Day of Spring

Palm Sunday

December 31
The Lord crowns the year with goodness!
Ps. 65:11

Good Friday

Have you ever noticed that the Bible talks a lot about lifting up your hands to the Lord? It tells us to lift up our hands when we're in the sanctuary and bless the Lord! (Ps. 134:2) The lifting of our hands is like offering a sacrifice to the Lord (141:2). We are to lift up our hands toward God's temple (that's in heaven!) (28:2); and when we think about the commandments of Scripture (119:48). We are also directed to lift up our hands in the name of the Lord (63:4). The Prophet Jeremiah says that lifting our hands symbolizes lifting our hearts to God (Lam. 3:41). And the Apostle Paul says that he wants people everywhere to pray, lifting up holy hands (1 Tim. 2:8).

Easter
He Is Risen!

Why do you think the Lord tells us to do that? I think it's so that we can see a picture of how our worship helps us let go of things around us so that we can let God take care of it. That's what happened to Rick Riso one day, and out of his learning to let go, God gave us a beautiful song!

April 21
Happy Birthday

Rick was driving to work one morning and it was already a bad day. The night before, someone had broken into his car. Not only had they stolen some things, but they had also broken the window and ripped up the dashboard. Now he was about to be late for work because he was stuck on the freeway in traffic. All the fumes from the other cars were blowing in through his broken window, and Rick was in a grumbly mood. It was just a rotten day.

April 30
Happy Birthday

In the middle of all of this, Rick heard the Lord say simply, "Worship Me."

Rick couldn't believe it! He didn't feel like worshiping right then! He felt frustrated, angry, and discouraged. "What do You mean!" He said to the Lord. "All of this stuff has happened to me! This is a frustrating day!"

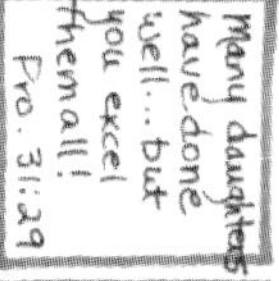
Many daughters have done well... but you excel them all!
Pro. 31:29

The Lord responded by saying, "If You will worship Me, I will give you a gift that will bless My people."

Mother's Day

Rick repented for his attitude and began to sing in worship to the Lord. (He couldn't lift his hands because he was driving, but he did the same thing in his heart . . . just like Lam. 3:41 says.) As Rick worshiped, the Lord gave Him the song, "Worship You."

May 28
Happy Birthday

The part of that song that I've always liked the best is the part that says, "Through all my days, I will give You praise." None of us ever knows what each day will bring us, and that's especially true as we go into a new year. Most days will be really good, although some days are likely to be what Rick's day was—frustrating. But as we remember the picture from the Psalms of lifting our hands to let go, we can let go of our frustrations and give them to the Lord. Then as we worship the Lord, He will do new things through us; new things that bless us . . . and everyone around us!

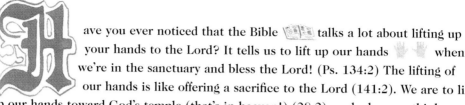

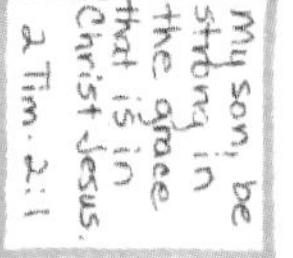
My son, be strong in the grace that is in Christ Jesus.
2 Tim. 2:1

Memorial Day

Vacation

July 24

July 4
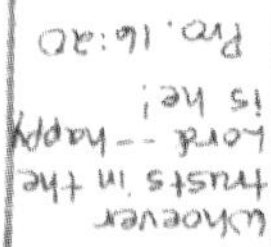
Whoever trusts in the Lord—happy is he!
Pro. 16:20
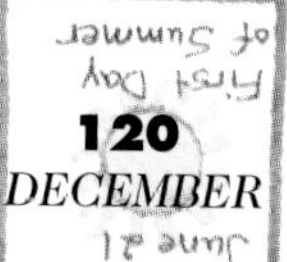
June 21
First Day of Summer
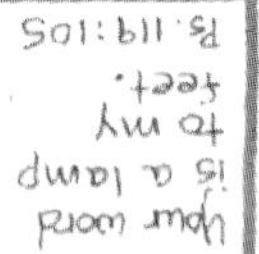
Your word is a lamp to my feet.
Ps. 119:105

Schools Out!

Father's Day

June 14
Flag Day!

Worship You

RR
Rick Riso
Wor - ship You, I will wor - ship
You here in this place, I seek Your face and wor-ship
You; Through all my
days I will give You praise Lord, in this
place my hands I'll raise and Lord I
wor - - - ship You.